Help Thou My Unbelief

Help Thou My Unbelief

by

Manford George Gutzke

THOMAS NELSON INC.
NASHVILLE / NEW YORK

Library of Congress Cataloging in Publication Data
Gutzke, Manford George.
    Help thou mine unbelief.
    1. Bible—Evidences, authority, etc.   2. Gutzke,
Manford George.   I. Title.
BS480.G83   248′.2 [B]   73–631

Contents

Help Thou My Unbelief

CHAPTER 1

Without Understanding

I have not always believed the Bible. I grew up with a very stubborn skepticism about the Bible. As a young man I thought that the Bible sounded like a gold-brick proposition. Parts of it sounded awfully good, but that was a long way from making it true.

Yet my lack of confidence in the Bible was not so much a matter of stubbornness, ill-will, or any settled opposition to what was in the Bible. My lack of confidence stemmed from my lack of knowledge and was confirmed in my lack of concern. I had no idea what was in the Bible. I had only a very vague notion of what it was all about, and I didn't care much. I was not a delinquent; I was not hostile or opposed to the Bible; rather I was merely unimpressed. My feeling about the Bible was very much the same as my feeling would have been toward a "Manual of Art Appreciation." A book on art appreciation might have been a very good book, but I would not have been especially interested in it. A "Handbook on Classical Music" could have been very reliable and very good, but I would not have been interested in that either.

Now, however, I have a total confidence in the Bible. I really believe it was written by "holy men of God" who "spake as they were moved by the Holy Ghost" (II Peter 1:21). I have not the slightest doubt but that "All Scripture is given by inspiration of God" (II Timothy 3:16). I accept the Bible without hesitation as the "only infallible guide and rule in matters of faith and practice," and I would be willing any time, anywhere, to be found following in the footsteps of Paul, the Apostle, "believing all things which are written in the law and in the prophets" (Acts 24:14).

In my childhood I remember we had a family Bible. I also remember the several times my father read in it. My family looked upon the Bible with respect. It was a "Church Book." I knew that the Bible dealt with God and about heaven, sin and hell. I went to Sunday School, and our Sunday School lesson was taken from the Bible. I memorized "The Golden Text," and it was found in the Bible.

When I was a child I felt that the Bible had some sort of magical power. Someone among our group of boys said that if you would put a key (an ordinary house key) at the point of a certain verse in the Bible, turn it any way you wanted to, ask a question about something that was very important, and leave the key there overnight, you would get a true answer. If your question was to be answered in the affirmative the next morning the key would have been turned over. That kind of thinking made the Bible a thing of magic, and I grew up looking at the Bible as a sort of good-luck piece. If you were to find a horseshoe in the road, opened toward you, you were walking supposedly right into good luck. A horseshoe, a wishbone, a four-leaf clover fall into the category of good-luck pieces, and I put the Bible with them. Somehow it might bring good luck.

Thus as a child I had a good bit of superstition in my mind about the Bible, but no real confidence. I might liken it to the way we felt about ghost stories. We respected it and feared it. It was everything that we would count sacred, like "Voodoo." But our feeling was, leave it alone; that was not one of the books with which we wanted to play.

When I was in grammar school I knew there were people who read the Bible. We did not generally read it in our home, but I knew some people read the Bible regularly. I thought reading the Bible was about like praying. There were people who prayed, but we did not. Some strange, queer folk would read the Bible and pray. Sometimes folks who wanted to be pious would read the Bible. Good people would read the Bible. If a man understood he was about to die, he would read the Bible. If some old lady had become an invalid, and could not do anything else or go anywhere, she would read the Bible. But for a man, healthy and well, to be carrying a Bible would have been like wearing a clerical outfit. I grew up in Canada where some preachers wore collars that fastened in the back, and some would wear a black vest that would cover everything. The Bible seemed to belong with that sort of thing. It was a symbol of piety; maybe it was a symbol of honor, of something good. Carrying a Bible would be like wearing a cross.

As a boy I knew that the Bible was used when people made an oath. When they went into court, they would be asked to swear on a Bible so that they would tell the truth. It had special meaning if they swore on the Bible. In those days we had a king in Great Britain. I remember the Coronation Day when the king was crowned. He had to take an oath of personal commitment when he assumed his office, and in taking his oath he put his hand on the Bible.

The Bible was to be respected like the flag. Our country's flag had its own personal history. Each color had a traditional story back of it. A great many people handle flags without knowing where they came from, and without knowing the reasons why they are red and white and blue, or why they have stars, or why they have stripes. For example, the British flag, The Union Jack, has various crosses on it. Each one of those crosses has a story. The flag has a history all its own. The actual production of the flag has a history, but I expect a great many people wave that flag who don't have any idea where it came from.

For me, the Bible was a sort of flag, the Christian's flag. I would honor it, and it never occurred to my mind that anyone ought to do anything disrespectful to it. I never had the idea that you should let a flag fall on the ground, and I would never have trampled the flag into the mud. I would have considered that a terrific insult to the people who cherished it. I felt the same way about the Bible. I would not have been satisfied to let anybody mark up a Bible or draw pictures in it, as if it were the funny paper. But yet, I didn't know anything about what was in it.

In high school I was an honor student. When I graduated I won a gold medal for the highest academic average. It could have been expected that I would have known why the Bible was so highly esteemed by good people. Yet as a teenager, my basic attitude toward the Bible did not change; if anything, there was a general deterioration in my appreciation of it. I still thought of it as something that might have some magic to it; I had times when I had a feeling of superstition about it; but generally speaking, I accepted it as a symbol of that which was good and true, without being interested seriously in its contents or meaning.

By the time I got into high school, I had read widely in English thought; and I found that most authors who quoted the Bible did so to bolster their own argument, whenever it suited their purpose. The authors I read did not attempt to show what the Bible said, but they tried to set forth that what they said was what the Bible supported. In other words, they would tell you what they had in mind, and then they would quote a passage of Scripture to show that the Bible said the same thing. This did not impress me, but it led me to feel that you could prove anything from the Bible.

I felt that the Bible should properly be thought of as a sacred book in our culture. I would have accepted the idea that it was an archaic relic of other days. I knew that the

Moslems had the Koran, the Buddhists had certain writings which they felt belonged to Buddha, and the Chinese had the writings of Confucius. Each of these countries had sacred books; and I regarded the Bible as another of such sacred books. I could concede that it may have been better than any of the others, but I didn't know. I did not know what was taught in the Koran; I did not know about the writings of Confucius; and to tell the truth, I did not know what was in the Bible either. The Bible to me was just another sacred book that had come down out of history. At best, it was a cultural item, something that belonged in our tradition.

While I was in high school, I felt that the Bible was woefully inaccurate and altogether out of date. I did not think anybody would have seriously thought the Bible was true as it is written. I thought that the Bible taught the earth was flat. I know now it does not, but I thought then it did. I thought the Bible taught that the world was square and that the sky was solid. It does not teach that, but at that time I thought it did. I thought the Bible was full of mistakes and that the historical items in it contradicted each other, and were not true to known facts. I thought that it was not scientific, and that it actually contradicted science. I would have made such statements as these without any hesitation, and I would have expected everybody to agree with me. I constantly heard statements similar to these, and I did not know any better; and you will remember I did not care much.

I accepted the Bible as a work of literature. I thought it was entitled to literary and poetic license. This thought was confirmed when I became aware of the big word *anthropomorphism*. This means that the Bible has a way of speaking about God as if He were a man. You may have heard that the Bible says "God walked in the garden." This seems to imply to some that God has a body like ours. In my youth, I thought that when the Bible spoke of God as a

person, that was "poetic license." It meant the same thing
to me as, when reading a poem, I found the ocean to be "a
great monster," or I found a mountain considered to be
"a great old man." The ocean is not a monster, and a
mountain is not a great old man, but poets can choose to
write in that way. I could have accepted the Bible in that
same way.

I thought that the Bible and its literature was fantastic.
The Bible speaks of angels! Now, who believes in angels?
That is like speaking of "ghosts." The Bible speaks of the
devil. Who would believe in the devil? That is just an idea.
And how silly to speak of demons! That was like speaking
about "brownies" or little "gremlins." In those days I
would just as soon have believed in gremlins as to have believed in demons. I knew the Bible talked about demons,
but then I felt the Bible was poetry, and such expressions
were to be taken as poetic imagination.

I felt that the miracles in the Bible were literary myth-
ology. I knew about the Greek myths and the Roman
myths. I read them and enjoyed them. The story of Jason
with the Golden Fleece was a great story. The tales of Hercules, and the story of Atlas holding the world on his
shoulders would thrill any young boy. I thought that the
Bible was a Jewish myth. The Bible stories were Jewish
stories, just like the Greek stories and the Roman stories.
Maybe the Jewish stories had a little more sense to them,
but still they were stories.

That was the way I grew up. I picked up this line of
thought from the people with whom I lived, the literature
I read, and the general treatment which I observed the
Bible to receive in the community. The stories in the Bible
were to me stories of folklore. I could read the story of
David, but I could also read the story of Jason and the
Golden Fleece. I could read the story of Moses, but there
was also the story of Hercules. I could read the exciting
story of the Exodus, but equally exciting was the Greek

story of the Odyssey. The Bible consisted of stories of a different culture, but it was just the same sort of thing, in my estimation.

Most of the fables that have been told in our day and time—stories such as "Red Riding Hood" and "The Three Bears"—all have some moral in them. I decided that the things written in the Bible were just fables or stories. I was not burdened about this; it did not bother me. This was my way of looking at the Bible. If anyone were to have questioned me, I would have pointed out, even with some sophisticated aplomb, that the Bible told about the creation of the world in seven days; but, of course, we knew that evolution accounted for the world. The Bible spoke about sin as something terrible man did against God, but actually the truth was that sin was just unfitness or imperfection or immaturity. The Bible even spoke about demons when men were sick, but everyone knew disease was caused by microbes. I would have said that the Bible was just pre-scientific.

If someone had asked me whether or not I thought the Bible taught morals, I would have said that the morals in the Bible were rather moldy. The Israelites obtained their Promised Land by destroying the inhabitants, the Canaanites. Some of the Israelites had several wives thus practising polygamy. I felt such thinking was outmoded.

In those teenage days I attended Sunday School and church. I went to Sunday School more often and occasionally taught a Sunday School class. In our church you could teach a Sunday School class without anybody asking you what you believed. It was a job to be done and I felt no aversion to doing it. I felt I was helping to get something done that would be done somehow by somebody. Somebody ought to do it. After all, I believed the Ten Commandments were solid. I had learned them as a boy and I liked them. Of course, they had things in them I did not understand, but when I read "Thou shalt not steal," "Thou

shalt not kill," "Thou shalt not bear false witness," I felt
those things were valid. I thought that the Golden Rule
was a good idea too. "Do unto others what you would have
them do unto you." I felt that if everybody did that, life
would be wonderful. Therefore, I went ahead and taught
with an easy conscience. I taught the Bible stories, not because they were true, but they were interesting stories, and
they comprised the lesson for the day.

Yet the Bible remained a closed book to me. It was just
a thing. It was something you might have on your desk. It
was something the preacher carried to the pulpit. It was
something to be used in courtrooms.

I had found out that many thinkers who seemed to be
honest and sincere had no confidence in the Bible. They
did not believe in ghosts. They did not believe in the devil.
They did not believe in hell. And so it was obvious to me
they did not believe in the Bible as being valid.

In my teenage days, I read the writings of one of the most
outspoken atheists that America ever produced, Robert
Ingersoll. I read his book, "The Mistakes of Moses." I read
it before I read Moses, and I was satisfied Ingersoll was
right. It sounded good to me. I read the satirists who
laughed at the Bible. I knew that the really smart men
poked fun at it. I knew that the *really* clever men like
Renan of France felt they had exposed its fallacies, and so
did others with whom I had become acquainted in my
reading.

Then, too, there were the critics. I found out about people who were working to expose mistakes in the Bible. I
had learned in school about the nebular hypothesis as to
the origin of the solar system, and I believed it. It sounded
good to me. It seemed that nobody took Genesis seriously
any more. I knew about the churchmen's opposition to
science. When Darwin's theory of evolution had finally
been presented, Huxley ran into opposition from the
church and in debate he made fools of the church people,

who opposed him. It did not mean much to me, though I did feel he should have been kind to them because, after all, they were just carrying on an old tradition. So far as the probable origin of man was concerned, I believed that evolution might be right and that man probably originated from some lower form of life. I would have told you that faith was like believing ghost stories. If you were going to believe in God, you could also believe in guardian angels, you could believe in all kinds of things if you wanted to. It was like magic.

There was actually no change in my thinking from my boyhood days all the way through high school. In time it became a comfortable alibi for neglecting to read and study the Bible. Also, it was getting to be a comfortable alibi for breaking the moral law, because after all *nothing* was authoritative. I had no reason to think I would ever have confidence in the Bible as a book of literature. I do not believe anyone could ever have persuaded me that the Bible was true. If the smartest people who believed the Bible to be true had been brought together, and had argued that the Bible was historically accurate, that it was scientifically sound, that it was psychologically true, or if they had argued for the reality of the person of God, the devil, of demons, of heaven, of hell, I think their arguments would have left me cold. Every time I had one question answered about the Bible, I could raise two more. The Bible was too vulnerable a book to be presented to the human mind for the human mind to believe it.

And to this day I feel this is still true. I would personally have no confidence in any atempt to persuade an unbelieving man by logic that the Bible is true.

Perhaps my feeling about this is grounded in my own experiences, but it seems there is ample empirical evidence to support this skepticism. Jesus of Nazareth commented on Peter's confession of faith, "Flesh and blood hath not revealed it unto thee, but my Father which is in heaven"

(Matthew 16:17). I know now from this statement that human argument and human reason will never be adequate to generate faith. But at that time in my life I did not know that—however, I did know that I was not being convinced, and felt in sad pessimism that I would never come to believe in anything which was resting on such an uncertain, and questionable basis as the Bible story.

I do not think I would ever have come to have confidence in the Bible if it had not happened that two conditions developed which together entirely changed my whole situation. I will describe these somewhat carefully in the next chapter, which will recount how I was helped in Providence to escape from the dead-end street of my own skepticism. I am not sure that I can recall clearly which of these developments occurred first, nor do I feel that I know what effect if any either had or has upon the other.

As I think back over my experience I realize that I became aware of a great need. It developed in me largely unconsciously, but somehow I began to realize that I was very, very sick. I was so sick, and I hurt so badly, that I would turn in any direction for help. Then someone came along and told me the Bible would cure me. When I then began to look at the Bible to see whether it would cure me, it was not because I was curious as to whether or not the Bible was accurate or true. The one thing that moved me to be interested in the Bible was a desire to know if there was really any way for me to be helped. Was there anything that could come into my heart that could help me? Was there any balm in Gilead?

I was especially affected by an inner loneliness that was absolutely devastating. It sapped all the strength out of my spirit. It seemed that nothing mattered.

In those days I would think if I were only an animal, then everything could go to wrack and ruin. What difference would it make? Farm animals were much better off than people. When I lived on the farm, I met many an animal whose personality and character I learned to appreciate more than some people I knew. I worked with some horses that were better gentlemen than some men I have come to know. I had some dogs of my own that were much better friends than those I found among people.

I thought man was in a miserable state: to have a mind and a heart such as he had, and nothing to show for it. It was when I became conscious of my need, when I became aware that I inwardly needed someone to be with me, that I found myself prepared for something.

At the time of my junior year in high school I had read widely and much, so that I was well aware of the common popular public opinion of religious matters. I do not say that I understood actually what religion was all about, but I had the feeling that I knew pretty well what people were thinking about such matters. My class-mates were ambitious to learn the facts of life and much of our leisure time spent in fellowship with each other was given over to discussion about the meaning of religion, of life, of God, of duty and of pleasure.

None of us knew what the Bible really meant; what could an intelligent, intellectual person believe about God; what is the reality indicated by such words as heaven, hell, angels, demons, God, Satan; or how could you be sure of anything. In our mutual conversations we would examine the witness of the older men in our community. Without being aware of what we were doing we examined the conduct of those in the community who were "the substantial, solid, good citizens" to learn what we *could* believe about all such matters.

When we considered the general practices in living followed by our most exemplary "guardians of our culture" we saw that though they all had Bibles, no one of them ever was known to read or to study or to use the Bible in any practical way. We drew the conclusion that they had no confidence in the Bible as a revelation of the present will of God.

And so in my youth I thought about the Bible very much as I would think about an old almanac. The Bible was woefully out-of-date, and it really didn't matter any more what was in it. It all had to do with past history. I doubt that I would ever have come to trust the Bible if I had just been approaching it as a book to be compared with other books.

Any arguments to support the Bible which might have been based on the findings of archaeology or historical research would have left me cold. And the study of the language would not have made a bit of difference in the world to me. Suppose someone had made a study of Homer's *Odyssey* and decided that two or three men wrote it instead of Homer. He would then have to figure out whether or not his conclusion was actually true. But it would not have made any difference to me, because I would not have been interested in his problem. And that is about the way I felt about the Bible.

CHAPTER 2

Without Hope

Something was happening to me personally which prepared me for a new and a different approach to the Bible. I developed a frame of mind that I will describe as unhappy depression. In miserable loneliness, I gave way to a cynical skepticism about all personal affairs. I had a feeling that nobody cared about me, and frankly I cared very little about them. A cold, realistic estimate about myself, my associations with the boys with whom I went around, and the people whom I knew prompted me to doubt that I had one real friend.

As I matured in self-consciousness, I began to feel personal guilt. I wasn't what I ought to be. My conscience reminded me that I hadn't always done what I should have done and that I had done some things I shouldn't have done. As I thought about it, I was appalled to realize that the character I maintained among the people in the community was actually a hypocrite's mask. I acted in courtesy and with respect toward others whom I actually despised for their faults and misdeeds. I was pleasant on the street with people whom I wished I had never met.

From what I could see, other people did the same. Men who told dirty stories when they were with other men would act gallantly toward women. To me that didn't make sense. Men who used profanity when they were with men would stand up in Sunday School and pray. As a result, I doubted everybody, and as a defense I isolated myself from others. This didn't mean that I thought I was better than they. Compared with others I knew, I might be a little stronger than some and a little smarter than some, but that was not the basis of my gloomy thoughts. I was painfully conscious of the evil in my heart. I knew when I was left to myself that my thoughts went wrong. I wasn't any good, and I began to suspect that others were not what they "pretended" to be. As I thought, I became more and more depressed by what I felt was the common deceit of mankind. It appeared to me that everybody was lying. I would have had no trouble at all endorsing the statement, "All men are liars," and I would have admitted that I was one of them.

In the same way and at the same time, I was infuriated by the occasional conceit of some people. That merely increased my general attitude of cynical rejection of people. Plagued by such miserable disillusionment and general despair concerning myself, I retreated into a general withdrawal from any confidence in anybody and that left me in aching, unhappy loneliness. Certainly in those days I would have said, "No man careth for my soul;" but since I did not care about anybody else, that left things about even, and I probably never gave it much thought. However, the loneliness was awful, and I was miserable.

Early in high school I remembered my mother. She had died when I was three and one-half years old. I remembered that the last time I had seen her, she was saying goodbye to me. As a boy three and one-half years old, I didn't know all that was going on, but I now remembered how she looked upon me with such a kindly smile on her face, and she had said that I was to come and be with her where she would be. During my childhood years I had forgotten about this. Then suddenly it came back to me, and I felt that if she had been alive she would have cared for me. She would have known all about me and would have loved me just the same. Not that she would have liked me, for I didn't even like myself; but she would have cared for me. I would have mattered to her. Then I asked myself, "Is she alive? If so, where? In heaven? But is there a heaven? There can only be a heaven if there is a God." I realized that I doubted the existence of God. I had come to the place where I really did not think there was a God.

I had become somewhat aware of the misery of mankind. I knew some horrible things had gone on in the history of the world; I knew innocent people had often suffered and weak people had often been robbed. If God was in control of all things and could have made this world any way He wanted it to be; and then He let things go on the way they were going, He must be a devil. These thoughts didn't trouble me too much, because actually evolution had my confidence. I figured that was the way the world came to be, and as far as men's sufferings were concerned I could accept them as being incidental to his growing. They were growing pains, rather bad, but after all, men had to grow.

Believing the theory of evolution was all right for the mind, but it didn't do anything for my heart. If that theory were true, we were all actually animals. Of course, men might be a little bit more sophisticated than other animals, but we were still just animals. I used to say to myself, living on the farm, that if we were just animals, the horses and the cows were ahead of us, for they had no inhibitions. They lived naturally. We abused them, we put them in their places and made them do what we wanted them to do; but still they didn't have to worry.

And so, as a high school boy, I thought men were just animals. Men might be just a little higher in the evolution scheme. At the same time, however, I asked myself, "Is this pessimistic view true? Am I just an animal? Is there nothing more to me than my physical body?"

I also asked myself, "Might heaven be real? Might my mother be alive? Might I have the chance to see her? Might I have the chance sometime to be with her?"

Perhaps you will think all my feelings were only psychological and that I had a "mother complex." I don't think that is what it was. I often thought what a wonderful thing it would be to have a friend, just any friend, somebody who knew all about me but loved me just the same. The people who knew me criticized me; they were always finding something wrong with me. I knew I needed criticizing, but I certainly would have appreciated a little kindness once in a while. I had the feeling that my mother would have been kind to me if she had been alive.

The question stuck in my consciousness: "Is she alive?" I didn't know. "Was it possible?" Yes, because I realized that while I didn't know *"yes,"* I also didn't know *"no."* While I didn't know there is a God, I didn't know there is no God. I could not say there is a God, but I could not say there is no God, either. Apparently, the whole business as to whether my mother was alive and whether heaven was real hinged upon the reality of God.

I was not aware of this particular Scripture at that time, but I was demonstrating it in my experience: "He that cometh to God must believe that He is, and that He is a rewarder of them that diligently seek Him" (Hebrews 11: 6).

Yet I couldn't believe that God was. When I realized that I could get no further in my thinking unless I accepted the idea that God is real, I was again in despair. Maybe He was real, and maybe He wasn't real. I was obliged in my own logic, therefore, to admit that maybe there was a God, maybe heaven was real, maybe my mother was alive, and maybe someday I could be with her, and I wouldn't have to be as lonely as I was, forever.

In those days, if I had met anyone who knew the Lord and had heard how the love of the Lord Jesus Christ is tenderer than a woman's love, I believe I would have received Him. I think I would have turned to Him just out of the desire to have someone care for me, but I didn't meet anybody that told me that.

One night I had gone out to get the cows from the field and was bringing them home to milk them. It was after dark, for dark comes early in the fall of the year in Canada. I was crossing a stubble field with the cows walking ahead of me. Above me was a starlit sky, and I was thinking over these things when suddenly I realized something. If God *is*, He sees me! I didn't know whether there was a God or whether there wasn't a God, but if there was a God I felt He knew me altogether. He knew my heart and mind.

With that thought before me, I was led to what I know now was my first real prayer. I stopped and looked up into the heavens, and I took off my cap. I felt like a fool. There might not be anything up there, but I was thinking that at least nobody was seeing me. I took off my cap just because there was a chance that God might be up there, and if He was I didn't want Him to think I was impudent.

I prayed something like this: "God, if you are up there, you know I don't know. You know I don't know for sure whether you are or whether you aren't. I don't know anything about it; but I will tell you one thing: if you are up there and if heaven is real and my mother is alive, and there is anything a person can do here on earth that would ever bring him to that place, if you will show me what to do, I will do it." As that seemed all there was to say, I put my cap on and walked away. Suddenly I was filled with a strange elation in my soul. I had a feeling I had been heard but, of course, I wouldn't let myself think that because it might be only self-hypnotism.

But something happened to me that night. When I went home, finished my chores and went to bed, I had a strange feeling of peace. I had entered into a deal with God if there was a God. If He would show me, I would come. That was settled.

As I thought about it the next day, I had a new problem. How would God show me? I was going to do whatever He said, but how would He show me? Would it be by a voice in the night? How much attention would I pay to hearing a voice in the night? I knew right well that if I heard a voice in the night I would think there was something unsound in my thinking; I would be having a mental disturbance. Would I get a message in a dream? If I had a vivid dream I would think it was something I ate the night before.

Would it be a vision? That would just be imagination. Would I see my name in the sky? The wind would blow the clouds around, and it would be gone. Would I see my name in the leaves on the ground in the forest? I wouldn't believe that. Would I see my name spelled out with sticks and stones? I would know someone had been there. Would it be events? Would I walk through a door and have something fall on me? That would depend upon how I interpreted it. I was actually frightened to realize that so far as God was concerned, if there was a God, I was incommunicado with Him. He couldn't get to me. How would He do it?

It dawned on me as a brand new idea that maybe that was what the church was about. I had stopped going to church. But now I planned to attend church regularly. Maybe God would move the preacher to say what I needed to hear.

Perhaps some of you may wonder why I didn't go to ask the preacher. I thought of that, but I decided that if I asked the preacher what I needed to know to get to heaven, he would just think up something to say to me. He would think of what he had read, and so it would be what other people had said. Or he would give me something that he had thought of, but that might not be the truth. Yet I felt that if that preacher didn't know that I was thinking about these things, and then he would get up and preach about them, I would have some reason to think that God actually was active in the process.

When I look back at that now, I am amazed that such thoughts came to me, as ignorant as I was. But from that time on, I went to church every Sunday. I mean I went to church to listen. I continued doing that for over three years.

After I had gone to church several Sundays, I said to myself, "This is too slow. Listening to a twenty-minute talk once every seven days, I might never hear what I need to know." I knew that the elation which I had felt because I had committed myself to seek the way to God, had begun to fade, and that frightened me. One day I might not even care, and that frightened me. I didn't know what to do.

Then the thought occurred to me that maybe this is what the Bible is about. I had a Bible, which I had received as a Sunday School prize for regular attendance some years before. I had not missed a single Sunday for one whole year. Of course, that wasn't because I was interested in the Bible or interested in Sunday School. All that meant was that I was healthy and my father had a strong mind and saw to it I went. But that very Bible which I received for having perfect attendance, was the Bible the Lord used in leading me to come to know Him.

I began reading the Bible. I undertook to read at least a chapter a day. I did it at night when I came in from work. When I had finished all my work and was supposed to have gone to bed, I would shut the door, light my coal oil lamp; and, lying there in bed beside that light, I would read at least one chapter, sometimes two or three, trying to find out anything that would show me how I could know the way to God. I read carefully. I had no superstitious hope that reading the Bible was going to be some magical thing such as if I read the Bible often enough something would happen to me. Rather, in a very practical, realistic way I was looking for guidance to heaven, and if that was to be found in the Bible, that would be fine. If someone had asked me if I believed what was in the Bible, I wouldn't have known what to say. I didn't know whether to believe it or not. Did I think those things recorded in there ever happened? I didn't know. That was not what I was after. I was trying to find out something that would lead me to know God, and I had gotten the idea that perhaps it was in the Bible, because the church used the Bible. Therefore, I read the Bible every day in the week and went to church on Sunday. I was looking for guidance.

Apparently I was reading with fairly close attention because I remember reading how the disciples asked the Lord Jesus, "Teach us to pray." He taught them the Lord's Prayer, and it struck me that it would be a good idea for me to memorize the Lord's Prayer. I added that to my ritual. Every night I read at least a chapter of the Bible, and when I was through reading I repeated the Lord's Prayer.

I also read that you couldn't please God unless you loved Him: "Thou shalt love the Lord thy God" (Luke 10:27). Then I read, "If ye love me, keep my commandments" (John 14:15). That seemed like something I could do. The only commandments I knew were the Ten Commandments, so I memorized them. I didn't understand all about them. The first one, "Thou shalt have no other gods before me," didn't bother me. I didn't have any god at all. I didn't make any image of God. "Thou shalt not take the name of the Lord thy God in vain." I had no trouble there. That was profanity, and my father wouldn't let me swear. "Re-

member the sabbath day to keep it holy." We kept the
Sabbath Day better than the neighbors. We were not
church members; they were, but we were more careful
about the Lord's day than they were. "Honor thy father
and thy mother." This one bothered me because I talked
back to my parents at times. I realized I would have to correct myself in that behavior.

Then I came to the practical commandments: "Thou
shalt not kill" and "Thou shalt not steal." I didn't want to
kill anyone, nor did I want to steal anything. Twice in my
boyhood days I had stolen something, and each time my
father had made me take it back. I had the feeling that I
could follow those things through.

My regular procedure every night became: reading the
Bible, at least a chapter, reciting the Ten Commandments,
and repeating the Lord's Prayer. On Sunday I went to
church and listened. I received no light but only experienced deeper despair. This continued for three years—
through high school, an extra year of post-graduate work,
and a year at home because I was too young to go out to
work. All the time I was keeping up my human ritual and
never seeing any kind of guidance.

While attending normal school preparing to teach, I
happened to visit a Presbyterian Church one Sunday night.
The sermon topic was "Heaven." This is it, I thought, now
I am going to find out. I had never heard anyone preach
on heaven. However, when the preacher finished his sermon, he said that some of the people there might be thinking that he hadn't told them how to get to heaven. That
was certainly what I thought, for he hadn't said anything
about it. "But," he said, "you all know who I am and
where I live, and if any of you really want to know how to
get to heaven, come and talk with me."

Two young men from the normal school were with me,
and as we left the church I told them that I was going to
fool that guy. He had said that if anybody didn't know the

way to heaven they should come and ask him, and I was going to ask him. They said they wanted to be there. So we made it a date for the following Tuesday night, when the three of us would call on the preacher in his home.

When we went to see the preacher, I told him we had heard his sermon, and I was the one who would like to know the way to heaven. I wanted him to tell me. I can sympathize now as I look back on that incident. I have been preaching now for a good many years, and I know that when a person asks a point blank question about spiritual things it can be disconcerting, especially when the preacher is not prepared to give an answer.

The preacher began to ask me about myself. He found out that I was going to be a school teacher. I lived a good life. I didn't drink, I didn't smoke, and I didn't carouse around. I didn't do anything that the public would call bad. I tried to be honest, I paid my debts, and so on. In addition to all that, I went to church every Sunday, I read a chapter of the Bible every night, I recited the Ten Commandments, and I repeated the Lord's Prayer. I remember how he said, "Why, you don't have anything to worry about. You're all right. You just keep on that road and you will get there."

We said goodbye, and when my friends and I got out on the street, I turned to them and said, "Ha, he doesn't know either." They wondered why I would say that, and I told them I had been going through that ritual for three years and there was nothing to it. Three years ago I had rung up the phone and had said to God, if there is a real God, "Show me." I had been holding that receiver to my ear ever since, but it was a dead wire. Although I went to church every Sunday, read the Bible every night, recited the Ten Commandments and repeated the Lord's Prayer, deep down in my heart I was more confirmed in my doubts than ever. I had no new impressions about the Bible.

In all the reading I did in that three year time, trying to

find out what the Bible meant, I skipped the long speeches and the histories in the Old Testament, and I overlooked the miracles. They didn't make any impression on me. I considered them cultural items of some sort. They were the kind of stories that belonged to a naive society. I passed by the queer morals and the strange ethics found in the Old as well as in the New Testament. They didn't particularly offend me, for after all, I lived with people, and human beings are capable of anything. I was looking and listening for some guidance which would bring me to God. It didn't matter much to me whether the Bible was true or not, but would it work? I had no particular hope. Rather, I had an expectation that the deeper I went into this the more I would find out that all is vanity. Why did I keep it up? I was the stubborn type, and I was still miserable in loneliness. Partly, I admitted that, in spite of everything, the answer might yet be there. Anyway, why not try it? There wasn't anything else to do.

CHAPTER 3

Without Answers

After I had been teaching school for almost a year, I made the acquaintance of an old farmer who had the country Post Office near my school. It was a four mile walk over to his place to pick up the mail on Monday, Wednesday and Friday evenings. The mail usually came in about 5 o'clock in the afternoon, and by the time I finished school at 4 o'clock and walked to the Post Office it was convenient for me to pick up my mail.

The farmer was an interesting person and because he was a widower living alone we had time to talk. Before long we began to talk about God. This old farmer was different from all the people I had met in that he talked as though he believed in God.

I suppose there were many among the people I met who believed in God, but they never showed it. They never acted like it and they never said anything about it. They certainly didn't say anything to me. I was wanting to find out, but nobody said a word to me, not even the preacher. I attended church on Sunday and heard the sermon, but when I met the preacher during the week he never talked about these things.

However, this old man believed in God. He believed that heaven was actually a place. His wife had died and he

thought she was in heaven. He believed in the Bible. He
had a Bible; he read it, and he looked to it for help. He
talked about these things and he told me the gospel without going into long explanations. It amounted to this: he
told me that heaven was real and that there was a free and
open way to heaven. A man could get there even if he was
a sinner. He quoted to me: "Whosoever will may come."

When I got this idea in my mind I was really startled.
Deep down in my bones I thought, "No sir, that's incredi-
ble." Afterwards, I wondered how he knew. Finally I asked
him how he was so sure heaven was free and how he was so
sure the way was open. He replied that that was what the
Bible said. Then I realized I had no confidence in the Bible. The fact that he told me it was in the Bible didn't
help me any.

Though I had no confidence in the Bible, I began to
think about it, for here was a man who had the very thing
I wanted. He had an assurance that he was going to heaven.
Although he was a widower, he talked about the fact that
he wasn't alone. The Lord was with him. That was the first
man I had ever met who talked that way, and I couldn't
quite make it out. He seemed to have good sense; he wasn't
a bad farmer; he managed well in his affairs.

From what I had found out in those several years living
on my own, generally the people who said they believed in
the Bible were good people. On the other hand I knew
people who didn't believe the Bible. Every little community has its atheist—somebody who has made himself ob-
noxious, and who is notorious for saying he doesn't believe.
When I compared these atheists with the people who did
believe the Bible, the people who believed came out far
better. This farmer seemed much superior in comparison
to the atheists I had met.

But if the Bible had something to say about going to
heaven, I felt I would have to find it out for myself. I was
sure it would not be as this farmer was telling me. I was

sure that I would have to work for it. You didn't get anything worthwhile unless you worked for it. So I began to
read the New Testament to check up on the old farmer.

It was my custom, you must remember, to read a chapter
in the Bible every night. That was always done privately.
But now I knew no good reason why I should go into a
room and shut the door to read my Bible. Was there something wrong with reading the Bible?

So one night after supper I took the Bible in my hand,
walked into the farm kitchen, opened the Bible and began
to read. I will never forget that night. There wasn't a person who said a word in that kitchen all evening. We just
sat there as if we were cut out of wood. I don't think I read
a word because of the emotional tension we were under. I
would keep asking myself, "What's the matter with this
Book? Why doesn't anybody want to read it?" After that
first time, every night, when we got through with supper
in the evening, I would go into my room, get my Bible,
come out and sit down to read in the place where I would
ordinarily sit with a book or a newspaper.

About the third night, the young man who lived in this
farm home said to me, "What's the matter? You going to
die?" I was surprised at myself when I said to him, "Well,
you don't know, maybe I will." I really hadn't thought of
that. When I was reading the Bible, I had no interest in
becoming pious. I wasn't trying to become good, and I
wasn't trying to do anything extra in the way of being
religious. Actually, I had no interest in the Bible as a book
in itself. All I wanted to know was, "Did it say that heaven
was real, as the old farmer said?"

I read a lot. I couldn't find where it would just really
say yes or no on the subject of heaven, but I kept looking.
I began to read in a special way. The old farmer helped
me. He gave me a set of proof texts to look up. It certainly
did sound as though heaven were real, and it did look as
though you could come to God by faith. That would be all
it would take.

I now came face to face with a big question. Even if I found that the Bible said the same thing as the old farmer, was that true? Was the Bible reliable? Can a man believe the Bible? I faced then what I see now are the classic problems.

As a young school teacher picking up a Bible, asking myself if this was true, I first of all thought of the text itself. I was aware of the fact that there were no original manuscripts. I knew that there was no one authorized manuscript to put your finger on and say, this is it. There are several hundred manuscripts taken together from which the New Testament has been derived, some copies different from others. I found out also they do not contain serious differences. They do not differ in the doctrines taught, but they differ in some of the things they include and some of the things they leave out. I realized, too, that there was no proof of authorship of the books of the Bible. You can accept the authors that are commonly given by tradition if you wish, or you can leave them out and have no author.

The Bible wasn't even written in English. It was written in Hebrew and Greek. Therefore, how did I know it was translated correctly? There were no supporting documents. If you read that certain things happened in the days of the Lord Jesus Christ, you couldn't read in some Roman history and find the same things because it would be hard to identify them. I decided that since all this had happened hundreds of years ago and nobody living today had ever seen it, I could never depend on any final verdict that would be reached by historical research.

No one could reconstruct the original. I don't say that because it is the Bible, but because it is history. As a student of history, one thing of which I am absolutely sure is that nobody can reconstruct any historical situation. There will always be factors that will be missed. Certainly no one at this distance could reconstruct what is reported in the Bible.

If it had been just a matter of picking up the Bible,
thinking about these things and realizing how little I knew
about it, I could have quit thinking about the Bible; but
there were people who did have confidence in it. I admitted
that. That raised the question: are these people who do
have confidence in the Bible liars when they say it is reliable, or are they fools that don't know any better?

But calling the folks I knew who believed the Bible liars
would make it the only thing they would be known to be
liars about. The folks I had in mind were men of integrity.
Should I call them fools? I wasn't so sure they were fools.
If they weren't liars and they weren't fools, where did that
leave me? If they were telling me the Bible was the Word
of God and really true, then I would be the one who would
have to believe it. And, you must remember, I didn't know.
But when you have said *you do not know for sure,* you
have admitted maybe *yes.* I used to say to myself, "Why
not just admit maybe *yes?"*

I asked the old farmer how he knew the Bible was true.
He said that the Bible was inspired, but I didn't know
what that meant. He explained that holy men of God spoke
as they were moved by the Holy Ghost. I wanted to know
who knew that. My friend said that was what the Bible
said, but I argued that that was what we were questioning.
If I am going to question a man because I am in doubt
about him and he tells me he is all right, his witness is of
no value. So how would I know? The farmer further
founded his claim by saying the Bible had been in the
church for over 2,000 years, and people had used it all that
time. Yet long usage was too uncertain for me. We had a
Bible in our home out on the farm but it didn't mean
much.

Finally I asked myself: what was the Bible supposed to
be and what was this book supposed to do? I admitted that
it was a book that apparently was to be offered as a means
to bring men to God—to show men the Gospel. That made

sense. The Bible could be in the world for a functional value. It was supposed to do something. It was to be like medicine. The only reason we have medicine is that, if we are sick, it will cure us. Its color and taste have nothing to do with its function.

Now I was on solid footing. If the Bible was a book that was supposed to accomplish something, then I could raise the question: does it do what it is supposed to do? If medicine is offered to me, I ask, "Does it or doesn't it cure?" If it does what it is supposed to do, it should be accepted as real and true. What was the Bible supposed to do? Was it supposed to show us the truth about Jesus Christ as the old farmer had said? I dismissed that because that could be poetic fiction. If some spiritually minded men got together and wrote about the Lord Jesus Christ and imagined all kinds of things about Him, were their writings true? I didn't know whether they were true or not. Was it supposed to affect men's lives? Yes. Has the Bible done it? Suddenly the phenomenon of Christianity came to my mind.

Remember, I was a school teacher and somewhat aware of the history of the world. I had read through Myers' *World History* when I was ten years old and found it as interesting as a story book. In fact, I thought it about two steps removed from Mother Goose Rhymes. When I read world history, I went through it with great zest because I was so interested in what happened elsewhere. I knew fairly well what was going on in the world, and now suddenly there came to my mind the phenomenon of Christianity. This became a sort of massive proof of the validity of the Bible.

People can say all they want to about how the Christian church has done this and that, and they can say how in the name of Christ people have done this and that; but take it all together through these 2,000 years and Christianity is real: it has built orphanages for homeless children, old folks homes for the aged, hospitals for the sick and schools for the ignorant. Christianity has made its way in the world; time is even dated from the birth of the Lord Jesus Christ. I found myself, as a school teacher, thinking about these things and admitting that Christianity was the greatest single sustained movement in history. Nothing had ever happened to compare with it. I have no doubt that the results of Christianity are far more impressive than what is mentioned in this paragraph. The reader must keep in mind I am giving some sort of report of the considerations I considered then, as I remember them now.

I am not talking about the total number of people involved. Starting out with a small handful of people, perhaps at the most as many as 500 at one time, in Judea, a captive province of the Roman Empire, among a subject people, the Gospel was revealed, and has spread and spread until it has gone around the world. If you tell me there are more Mohammedans than Christians or more Buddhists or followers of Confucius than there are Christians, I will tell you that those particular religions have a peculiar national and cultural character. The amazing thing about Christianity is that it has moved across every ocean, over every mountain, through every forest, and across the burning sands of deserts from one culture to another. It has broken into every land. It is repeated in over a thousand different languages. It touches all levels of society—the rich and the poor, the old and the young, the learned and the unlearned, the people who are in charge and the people who are slaves.

Even in the days when I was an agnostic and didn't believe, I had to admit that, so far as history recorded, wherever Christians were talked about they were alike in their fruits. They showed charity, more virtue than other people, and more integrity. There was a difference in these people compared to others in the world.

I knew what Voltaire had said about the Bible. He said that seventy-five years after he was dead no one would read it. But I was reading it; I knew too that the Red Cross was known all around the world for showing mercy, and the symbol of the Red Cross was taken from Calvary. These things began to press upon me. I began to recognize that Christianity and the Bible were inseparably related. I asked myself if there would be Christianity without the Bible. Could the Bible be operative anywhere without Christianity?

I had to admit it was something like this: if you put some wheat grains in the ground, you may have some wheat. Wherever wheat grows, it comes from wheat seed which has been put into the ground. If the seed is put in the ground, the grain will grow. That would mean that the wheat seed put in the ground and the wheat plant which grows out of the ground are inseparably related. I argued it out that way for my own satisfaction until I felt it was scientifically demonstrated that the Bible is the seed of Christianity.

Wherever you find Christianity being launched, someone is teaching the Bible, and wherever you find Christianity with any strength, you will find someone is reading the Bible. Those two things are inseparable. There was no doubt about Christianity. No matter how skeptical a man is and no matter how much fault he finds with Christianity, he will have to admit that Christianity is a real phenomenon. If the Bible is related to Christianity that way, then the Bible must be real.

But is it true or false? I didn't know, but I would ask myself this question: can a lie promote virtue? That didn't seem logical to me. On the basis of the testimony of Christianity, I was able to accept in my mind that the Bible is real and that it is effectual—not because I knew what was in it, for I didn't know what was in it; but because I had to admit its power. Following this line of thought, I admitted to myself that if the God of the Christians is real, then the Bible is His revelation. If there was

a real God and Christians were really His people, He
wouldn't let them be fooled with any hoax. If it wasn't
true, there would be ways to find that out. Christian people
believed in a God whom they affirmed, and they took the
Bible as their book. This all seemed tied up in such a way
that if there was a God at all then the Bible was His revelation.

It was on a bridge, out in a country community north of
Gilbert Plains, Manitoba, one Sunday afternoon in broad
daylight that I suddenly realized that for me if there was a
God at all the Bible was His book. I didn't even know what
was in it, but I knew that if Christians come from God,
have dealings with God, and go to God, then the book of
the Christians, which is the Bible, would be the book that
God allowed them to have that would lead them toward
Him. Though I still doubted the reality of God, I felt sure
about the reality of the Bible. I didn't get the reality of the
Bible by reading it and by hearing arguments about it. I
understood the reality of the Bible from Christians, the
testimony of Christianity.

I now began to look at the Bible in a new way, and I
asked the question: how does the Bible affect men to pro-
duce such results? My own conclusion was derived from
general events. I took Christianity as a whole. Would there
be any Christianity if there weren't personal individual
Christians? Would there be any such thing as Christianity
if there were not individual instances of people becoming
Christians? Which would come first? Apparently the Christian comes first. Paul is before the church is. Paul preaches
and the church comes into being.

Christianity extends beyond the church, and it isn't all
from God. Much of what we have in Christianity is just
human, but Christianity is the splash that is made when
the Gospel is dropped into the ocean of mankind. It is the
shadow that is cast when the Gospel is held up on the
horizon of mankind. The whole community might be in-

fluenced as I was, but there must be some origin or it
would die out. You can get momentum in the community
as a whole, but somewhere there must be a real dynamic.

It seemed natural that one should become a Christian
because of the Bible. I had no trouble with that, but how?
I kept reading the Bible. I talked with the old farmer, and
I thought it out. The answer was by believing the promises
from God that are in the Bible. I could easily have quoted
this verse: "For by grace are ye saved through faith; and
that not of yourselves: it is the gift of God: not of works,
lest any man should boast" (Ephesians 2:8-9). The problem had been worked through to this point: man on earth
could come to God (the God of the Bible) and he could
belong to the God of the Bible if and when he believed
what the Bible said. How could a man honestly, intelligently believe in something he did not know to be true?
That was my problem.

At this point my own reflection was focused upon the
problem of believing, not so much any specific item in the
Bible, but rather, the Bible as a whole. How could I believe? Granted that the Bible is real, as Christianity is real,
and it is effectual, because Christianity does come to pass,
and granted that the effect of the Bible is good, because
Christianity when it has its normal character is good, and
understanding that if it is to influence the group as a whole
it must be accepted by individuals and if I am one such
individual, how can I believe in something that I do not
know? How can I know unless I try it out, unless I put it
to the test, and unless I believe it? But, how can I test it if
I don't know it?

Someone would say you can believe it hypothetically,
tentatively; but would that be a real test? Do you really
believe it unless you put yourself into it? For instance, if
you want to find out whether or not a bridge will hold you,
will you really find out if you just look at the bridge? Will
you really find out if you just lean over and put one toe

on it? You won't find out whether the bridge will hold you until you put your weight on it. You have to move out onto the bridge if you are going to find out if the bridge will hold you. But by the time you have moved out on the bridge, you have already taken the risk.

I don't think I understood what "believing in" actually meant. Somehow I thought "to believe" and "to know" were the same. Of course, they are not the same. If you knew, you wouldn't have to believe. You may believe certain things, and the reason you exercise faith in them is because you do not know everything about them. I found I was holding to the idea that it is not intelligent to believe in something about which it is possible to have doubts. Because I could doubt the Bible, I couldn't believe it; and because I couldn't believe it, I couldn't become a Christian. At that time in my own personal affairs I was stymied, as it were, behind my doubts. I was still hurting; I was still miserable; I was still intolerably depressed. I would have been ready to forget the whole problem as something I could never figure out and throw myself with abandon into Epicurean living, which is to eat, drink and be merry, for tomorrow we die; but maybe it was true! And already I had invested so much. Should I now not see it through? After all, I had been spending a long time trying to find out.

That is the point at which I began to take another turn in my thinking. I began to doubt my doubts because I found out that my whole attitude toward the Bible and toward God was conditioned by my doubts and that I was putting much trust in my doubts. I began to wonder if I was wise to doubt as I did.

CHAPTER 4

The Experience of Believing

At this stage I counted the Bible as a cultural item of great importance. I considered the Bible as the source of the dynamic of Christianity. The things that made Christianity different from other religions were directly related to the Bible. Although I did not know what was in the Bible, I couldn't deny the significance of Christianity in the world, and that made the Bible important. There was a tone of morality, an aspect of decency, and a wide-spread character in Christianity, just as in some other cultures, that probably made the Bible a good book. I was able and willing to believe all that; but I couldn't accept the Bible as the Word of God, as something of superhuman origin.

As yet, I did not seriously examine the Bible to see what it had to say for itself. I had the attitude that if I were doubting a man's integrity, I wouldn't ask him to tell me about himself. After all, how could I accept the testimony of a man about himself if that man's integrity were in question?

Then I found that I began to doubt my doubts. Suddenly I realized that I was actually entrusting my soul to my skepticism. I didn't want to put any confidence in faith, but I put all my confidence in myself. I didn't have the faith to come to God, but I had the doubt to stay away from God. I realized I was putting more confidence in my doubts than I was putting in whatever Christianity stood for. I now began to question whether or not that was intelligent. Was it a valid principle to doubt as long as possible before believing a thing?

At this time I was teaching school in northern Manitoba and boarding in a farm home. I asked myself if this would make sense: the food served at the table by my landlady might have been poisoned. Who knew that it wasn't? There had been cases of ptomaine poisoning. Because sometimes food was poisoned, would it be an intelligent thing for me to suspect all food unless it had been examined? Would it make sense if I made it a rule that the food had to be chemically analyzed before I would eat it? This would mean I would have to trust the druggist who would be examining the food. Suppose the druggist was a liar; then where would I be? Really, I had no way of establishing that the food I was going to eat at the next meal was free from poison. How would I know?

If someone were giving me change in a store and handed me a five-dollar bill, would it be an intelligent thing for me to ask if the money had been certified by the bank? There are counterfeit bills, and I could think this particular bill was such. Was it an intelligent thing for me to doubt because it could be doubted?

I was treating the Bible exactly that way: as long as I could doubt it, I would. If I got to the place where I wouldn't eat my food unless some chemist analyzed it, and I wouldn't accept a five-dollar bill unless a banker certified it, it dawned on me that someone would probably be looking for me with a net. They would think I was insane. Yet that was exactly the way I felt about the Bible. Should I demand an on-the-spot test before I would accept anything? That was the mark of an unbalanced mind.

At this time I was planning to study law, and I was reading a book on the laws of evidence as given in court. In order to establish any item as a legal fact in court, it only has to be proven beyond reasonable doubt, never beyond possible doubt. Nothing can be proved beyond possible doubt, no matter how one tries to prove it; for some possible reason for doubting it can ultimately be found. That made sense to me.

When I reflected on it I asked myself this straightforward question: is it reasonable to doubt the Bible? If I don't doubt it, what am I supposed to do? Am I supposed to trust it? But what does it mean to trust the Bible?

What does it mean to trust anybody? What does it mean to trust a doctor? Under what conditions will I go to a man who is a stranger to me, let him examine me thinking whatever thoughts he has in mind, and let him prescribe for me certain medicine which I do not understand? I will take his prescription to the nearest drugstore, and the druggist will go into his laboratory where I haven't been and where most of the bottles are marked with "skull and crossbones" and the word "poison." He goes out of sight from me, works fifteen or twenty minutes, comes out with a box of capsules, and I am to take one before each meal. What is in those capsules? I don't know, but I pay the price and take them home. Is it intelligent for me to swallow those capsules? I don't know what is in them. I wasn't there when the druggist compounded the prescription, and if I had been I wouldn't have known what he was doing. I don't know what the various drugs mean. I don't know what the doctor thought. I could doubt three or four different steps along that whole process. Would it be reasonable for me to refuse to take that medicine, because in my ignorance I could doubt that it would be helpful?

Why is it intelligent for me to go to a stranger, to have him do this to me? Because he is a doctor. What does that mean? It means that he has taken the prescribed course, he has passed the examination, and has been licensed to practice. More than that, it means he has patients who trust his judgments.

Some years ago I went to a doctor for the only time I have ever had surgery. The surgeon was a complete stranger to me. After he examined me, he rendered me completely helpless by the use of anesthetics. He strapped me down on a table so I couldn't move, and then he cut into me. None of that was vicious. It was all good, and I paid him for it. Would it have been intelligent for me to stop him because I didn't trust him? Why did I trust this man whom I had never seen before? I trusted him because another doctor, a good friend of mine, recommended him to me.

You don't always trust people because you *know* them. You sometimes trust people because you *know about* them. After you have had your own experience, you can testify; but until you have had your own experience, you can't testify. Look again at that bottle of medicine you picked up from the druggist. Under what conditions would you trust it? If it had been prescribed by a responsible doctor and prepared by a responsible druggist, it would be the intelligent thing for you to believe that the medicine will be all right. In other words, it would be safe beyond reasonable doubt. There might be a slip-up or a mistake, but not beyond reasonable doubt.

Another illustration occurred to me back in those days. Suppose I am driving along the road in my car, and I come to a suspension bridge over a deep canyon. As I look at that bridge, it doesn't look strong enough to hold a car. It looks as if all it can do is hold itself up. I drive up close to its approach and stop. I even get out and look at it. By merely looking I can't tell you whether that bridge will hold me or not. I am not an engineer, and I don't know where the supports are buttressed in the water of the river or at the edge of the canyon. I don't know how much strain it will hold. Will it be intelligent for me to drive across that bridge?

While I am sitting there wondering if the bridge will hold us, a man driving a big truck with a load of gravel stops beside me. He inquires why I have stopped and if I am in trouble. I tell him I have to get to the other side of the canyon, and I am wondering whether to cross the bridge. He asks me what my problem is and why I don't go. I tell him I don't know whether the bridge can hold me or not, and I'm afraid it might collapse. The man assures me that bridge won't collapse for he drives over it every day, and he is going to take a load of gravel three times as heavy as my car over it right now. Wouldn't it be intelligent for me to drive over the bridge if he had been over it with his big truck? The matter of confidence in anything or anybody, trusting anything or anybody, would depend upon the witnesses, the people who tell you, the people who make clear to you what will happen.

When I reached that point in my thinking, I asked myself if I knew somebody who had actually tried the Bible. If I knew someone who believed it, I might conceivably have a witness; and I could find out if it really did work in his case. I remembered that back in the home community where I was reared there was a man who believed in the Bible, and his actions reflected his beliefs. There were others who, I am sure now, believed the Bible; but I didn't know that for certain. There was no special evidence that they believed the Bible. This particular man, however, did an unusual thing. At a certain time in the church year a special offering was taken for foreign missions. The offering was usually quite small. On this particular occasion when the offering for foreign missions was received, this man personally contributed more money than the rest of the church. In fact, he put more money in than I thought anybody would ever give to missions. That impressed me a great deal.

Why would he give to missions? He had never been to South America, Africa, or India. Why would that man living in North America, in Canada, give to missions? Why would he care? It was because he believed the Bible. When the rest of us were giving fifteen or twenty-five cents and considered it a good contribution, this man gave a generous gift to missions. In fact he gave forty dollars. It was not because he had to, nor because it was expected of him, but because he sincerely wanted to. Mr. Carruthers, a simple farming man, read the Bible, knew something of what was in it, and believed it. It actually made a difference in his life.

During this time, although I was reading a chapter of the Bible every day, I was not studying it to know what it really meant. Thus I looked to the only man I personally knew who actually used the Bible and said it was good and real. There was my witness and evidence.

While this was going on in my mind, the country postmaster, with whom I had regular discussions, taught me the gospel. I knew the outline: (a) Christ Jesus died for sinners; (b) anybody believing in Him would be saved. I understood that. The postmaster had given me the Scripture references to show that that was what the Bible taught, and I had checked them. I was satisfied that the Bible taught what the old man said was the gospel. But did I have the evidence that the Bible was real and good? Could I accept that the Bible was real because Christianity was real? I now had the evidence that the Bible was good because our neighbor, Mr. Carruthers, who believed it, was good. But could I accept it as the Word of God? If I were going to accept it as the Word of God, I would have to believe that God is, and that was the very thing I doubted.

This then, became my problem. Is there a God? Does He care? Can He do anything? I thought about certain lines of proof concerning the existence of God. I decided that if those lines of proof were met I really could believe. Within two weeks those very proofs, to which I had myself agreed, undeniably appeared. The result was a great experience in my soul that brought me to believe that God is. From the moment that I believed that God *is,* and "is a rewarder of them that diligently seek Him" (Hebrews 11:6), I had no difficulty in accepting the Bible as the Word of God. I had Christianity, and I had a man like Mr. Carruthers to support my confidence in it.

Rapidly it became clear to me that the gospel which the old postman taught me and showed me in the Bible seemed really true. If there was a God, then God would have given us the Bible as a means of accomplishing the work of bringing people into His presence and guiding them into His will. I connected the two things together. When once I was convinced that God *is,* I was soon convinced that the Gospel is really true.

Shortly after I had recognized this, I was given grace to believe in Jesus Christ and to accept Him, and I was gloriously blessed to be an adopted child of God. I commonly refer to that as my conversion. I often talk about it as coming out of darkness into His marvelous light. My heart was filled with praise to God for His grace.

When I had this experience of accepting the Lord and putting my trust in Him, I cherished the Bible. I loved the Bible because it was the source of the Gospel. It preserved the record of Christ Jesus who was now my Savior and Lord. I still didn't know what was in the Bible. I hadn't really studied to find out whether or not I accepted as true all the things that were in it, but I knew what it did. I knew that it was the source of the Gospel which I had learned from the postmaster. It was the source of the Gospel that was believed by Mr. Carruthers who gave money to missions. I knew it was the source of the Gospel which had produced Christianity.

CHAPTER 5

Beginning at Moses

Some time after I became a Christian, my attitude toward the Bible presented a baffling aspect. If ever I had an unreasonable frame of mind, this was the time. I accepted the Bible as the book of Christianity; and because Christianity was real, I judged the Bible to be real. I accepted the Bible as the source of comfort for all Christians. And because Christians were sincere, true people and were comforted by the Bible, I was encouraged to believe it must be a good, true book. I accepted the Bible as the source of the gospel.

The gospel had been used to bring me to the Lord Jesus Christ, and I appreciated it very much. I highly regarded the Bible because that was where the gospel came from. I accepted the Bible as the revelation of God's plan. I really thought that if anyone wanted to know what God wanted to do, that person should read the Bible and he would find it there; but still I did not want to accept every part of the Bible. There were some things in the Bible I felt I could not believe.

I continued reading the Bible. I cherished it, I appreciated it; but I did not believe what it said in some of its accounts. I didn't believe the Old Testament. Being "old" would mean that it wasn't any good. Didn't it say somewhere in the New Testament that the old was taken away that the new might be put there? I didn't think I was missing anything when I didn't believe the Old Testament. I considered the Old Testament as a sort of historical prelude. It was something through which the gospel finally came to pass. I didn't make any great study of it, and I certainly didn't have any confidence in it.

The miracles in the New Testament and certainly those in the Old Testament embarrassed my scientific frame of mind. I just skipped over them.

I read the story of the virgin birth. I wouldn't have criticized anything about that because it was about the Lord Jesus Christ, and anything honoring Him would have to be considered as all right. But I didn't really believe the virgin birth. With reference to the opening of the Red Sea, I thought that the wind blew to open it. When the Bible stated that the waters of the River Jordan were piled up above and below, I didn't really believe that. I didn't really believe the Lord Jesus walked upon the water —it just looked as though He were walking on the water. I generously allowed that the writers of the Bible were writing in pre-scientific days to people with naive imaginations. They filled in their stories and made them sound good.

I did believe in the resurrection. I really did take that to heart. I believed in the ascension, astonishing as it was, because I had to believe the resurrection and the ascension to be saved. Paul said, "That if thou shalt confess with thy mouth the Lord Jesus, and shalt believe in thine heart that God hath raised him from the dead, thou shalt be saved" (Romans 10:9). And so I had to believe it in my heart to be saved; I did and it was a shocking experience. My coming to faith (to believe in the miracle of the resurrection and to accept the ascension) still left me wondering. I accepted it, but that was all.

The result was (and I hope I can say this without giving anyone the wrong impression) that I was gloriously saved in a remarkable fashion before I believed the virgin birth to be true, before I believed in the miracles of the New Testament, and before I believed the Old Testament. I say this to show how wonderful God is. I decided to go to the mission field, and I was actually on my way before I believed in the Old Testament. Someone may say, "But you believed the Bible." Yes, I believed the Bible. "How can that be?" I don't know, and I have often said since that the mind of man is a strange mixture of contradictions.

The Bible as a whole was the medicine which I took to cure myself. And because it cured me, the Bible as a whole was authentic. I was ready to think, however, that the Bible as a whole contained foreign particles. This was the medicine that cured me all right, but it had some impurities in it. I would have been ready to think that the Scriptures were the ore that had to be refined by critical, intellectual processes to get the truth out of it. You would take the ore, put it into the crucible of your own mind and heart, and by critically examining it bring out of it the refined gold, silver and various precious metals. I would have thought that there were certain parts of the Scripture that could be considered as ash piles from the fires of devotion that had burned in the hearts of certain men. I didn't hold it against Elijah that he had left a few clinkers around (some of the miracles he had performed.) The important thing was that his heart was really and truly confident in God, and he left a great record of the things he had done for God. I would have been quick to say to you, just as much as anyone would today, that the literature of the Bible represents the earthen vessel wherein is the doctrine of truth. I have heard that kind of statement so often that I can say it backwards and forwards.

I was perfectly ready to think of the Bible as you think of an orange. You peel the orange and then you eat it. I was ready to peel the Bible and then take out the truth. We don't eat the peelings.

But now I have total confidence in all the Scripture. This attitude grew in my believing heart until today I have confidence that the Scriptures of the Old and New Testaments are true and without error.

In reporting how I came to this total confidence, I will not attempt a narrative account in chronological sequence because I am not sure I could remember. I think I carried two, three, or four questions in my mind at all times, and they only came to the surface from time to time.

One of the first problems that I had to deal with was the matter of the validity of the Old Testament. I have already mentioned this. The validity of the Old Testament never did loom as a problem of my faith. I wasn't concerned whether or not Genesis or Exodus and the stories of Elijah, Elisha and Daniel were true. They didn't enter into my concern. I had accepted the Gospel of the Lord Jesus Christ as it was preached by Christians. I had accepted Him, and I understood that Christians got their ideas from the Bible. But that didn't mean they believed everything in it. My faith related me to Jesus Christ. In Him I was saved and I felt that was all that really mattered.

I was studying the Bible at the Bible Institute of Los Angeles on my way to the mission field when I came face to face with the matter of the validity of the Old Testament. In order to pass my courses there I had to read and study the Old Testament. That raised important questions. Is it true? Did these things really happen? Did the Lord God actually say these things?

From all that I could read in the New Testament it would appear that Jesus of Nazareth believed the Old Testament. Nobody could read Matthew, Mark, Luke and John and have any question that Jesus believed it. He quoted it, and when He quoted it, He quoted it without correction. He never once said that the writing of David should be changed, that the writing of Jeremiah wasn't true, that the writing of Micah shouldn't be understood the way in which it was written, or that this writing of Moses was not what it says. Every single time He quoted the Old Testament He quoted it as if it had authority. It answered questions, settled problems, and ended discussions. Jesus would refer to the events and the miracles in the Old Testament without ever toning them down.

How surprised I was when I came to add it up. Almost every miracle that was doubted in the Old Testament the Lord Jesus referred to in the New. Concerning the flood, He said, "But as the days of Noah were, so shall also the coming of the Son of man be" (Matthew 24:37). "And as it was in the days of Noah, so shall it be also in the days of the Son of man" (Luke 17:26). He referred to the destruction of Sodom and Gomorrah (Mark 6:11). He used the Old Testament against Satan. When He was tempted of Satan, He answered, "It is written" (Matthew 4:4, 7, 10). He was the Lord, and if anybody could have originated a better statement, He was the One to do it. Yet when He confronted Satan and refuted him in His three big temptations, He quoted Scripture every time. And He used it *exactly* as written.

Another thing of interest to me occurred after the resurrection of the Lord Jesus. While He was here upon earth, He was God Himself in human form. Certainly, if anyone could have known the mind of God in any better way than the prophets of old, it would have been Jesus Christ. But after His resurrection from the dead, He opened His disciples' understanding that they should understand the Scriptures. The Scriptures in existence then were the Old Testament Scriptures. The account goes on "And beginning at Moses and all the prophets, he expounded unto them in all the scriptures the things concerning himself" (Luke 24:27). The Lord Jesus used those things to present the meaning of His resurrection. He opened their understanding that they might understand the Old Testament Scriptures.

I remember how that affected me. I was shocked to think that I didn't even know what the prophets said. The Lord Jesus told what *"all* the prophets" had said about Himself, and I didn't know what it was. It gave me a strange feeling of inadequacy. One of the results was that I began reading the Old Testament right away. Maybe the Holy Spirit wanted to show me something and couldn't because I didn't even know the material. If I knew the Scriptures, the Holy Spirit might be able to interpret them for me.

From the day I realized that the Lord Jesus believed the Old Testament, I have never had a very serious doubt about the Old Testament Scriptures myself. There are many things I don't understand, but if you ask, "Do I trust them?" my answer is, "Yes, I do." If you ask me why, the first thing I will tell you is that when the Lord Jesus Christ was here He had practically the same material, word for word, in His hands and He did not change any part of it. I thought about Paul. When Paul was in court and on trial for his life, he told them that ". . . after the way which they (his critics) call heresy, so worship I the God of my fathers, believing all things which are written in the law and in the prophets" (Acts 24:14). He wasn't saying "all things *meant by* the law and the prophets," or "believing all things you can *derive from* the law and the prophets," or "believing all things that the law and the prophets can be used for." He was saying, "Believing all things that are *written in* the law and the prophets."

When the Apostle Paul stood before Agrippa again, on trial for his life, we find him saying, "Having therefore obtained help of God, I continue unto this day, witnessing both to small and great, saying none other things than those which the prophets and Moses did say should come" (Acts 26:22). Thus Paul the apostle stood in the court of King Agrippa and claimed that he had been teaching and preaching only the things that the Old Testament sets forth and encourages us to believe. When Paul was writing to the

Romans, he said, "For whatsoever things were written aforetime were written for our learning, that we through patience and comfort of the scriptures might have hope" (Romans 15:4). In 1 Corinthians 10:11 he states, "Now all these things happened unto them for examples: and they are written for our admonition, upon whom the ends of the world are come." These things would bring to our minds that Paul personally considered the Old Testament to have been written especially to help us.

When writing to Timothy, Paul had this to say: "All scripture is given by inspiration of God, and is profitable for doctrine, for reproof, for correction, for instruction in righteousness: that the man of God may be perfect, thoroughly furnished unto all good works" (II Timothy 3:16–17). There it is in a nutshell: "All scripture is given by inspiration of God." At the time Paul was writing, the Old Testament was the main portion of Scripture in the hand of any believer.

There are other New Testament apostolic evidences. In 1 Peter 1:10–12, talking about the salvation which God provides in Christ Jesus, Peter says that the Old Testament prophets searched in themselves diligently "what or what manner of time the Spirit of Christ which was in them did signify, when it testified beforehand the sufferings of Christ, and the glory that should follow" (1 Peter 1:11). The Old Testament prophets were seeking to know about the Lord Jesus Christ, "unto whom it was revealed, that not unto themselves, but unto us they did minister the things, which are now reported unto you." They wrote down the things they were led to write so that we might learn from them now in this day and time.

Peter uses the Old Testament Scriptures and suggests that they are actually revealing the Gospel to us. In II Peter 1:21 Peter says, "For the prophecy came not in old time by the will of man: but holy men of God spake as they were moved by the Holy Ghost."

Over and over again, the New Testament uses the Old Testament as it is written and without change. It uses it with every confidence, never questioning what was written. All the problems of the miracles in the Old Testament were known in the time of the apostles, but the apostles did not change these stories. They did not leave any part out.

So far as I was concerned, all of this added up to just one thing: the Old Testament was believed by the New Testament. From that time on I proceeded to read it. I couldn't get away from the fact that if the Lord Jesus had been talking to me and had begun at Moses, the Psalms, and all the Prophets to refer to all the things concerning Himself, I wouldn't have known what He was talking about. I hadn't even read those Scriptures.

Another problem that came up was the matter of the authenticity of the miracles. For a long time when I was a young Christian, the miracles just embarrassed me—sometimes even annoyed me. I thought it was too bad they were in the Bible because they made it so hard to believe. To me the miracles were like fish bones; they would just stick in my throat. I accepted the general idea that you didn't have to believe them. You could explain them away.

As I faced the problem of the miracles, I found that my first objection arose because miracles did not follow the usual pattern. A miracle takes place in a way that is different from the way in which things ordinarily happen. Thus the common reaction would be that a miracle is impossible. When I faced that problem and asked myself if it truly were impossible, I was impressed by Gabriel's words to Mary when he announced the virgin birth to her. She asked, "How shall this be?" (Luke 1:34). And he said, "With God nothing shall be impossible" (Luke 1:37).

When the Lord Jesus was talking to the disciples and Peter asked Him, "Who then can be saved?" He said, "With men it is impossible, but not with God: for with God all things are possible" (Mark 10:26–27). So the argument against the miracles being authentic just on the basis of their being impossible isn't valid. What then is impossible for God to do?

A more serious question is this: do the miracles as they are presented violate God's law? God's law has certain uniformities of consequence, certain uniformities that appear in all things that happen. A miracle is different; therefore, I asked whether or not it violated God's law.

But is God's law so rigidly uniform? Is it God's law that everything must happen always in exactly the same way. If God is a living Being, couldn't He change it? If God is a living Being, couldn't He withhold the pattern for the time being?

We have been so much inclined to think that natural law prevails that we would be surprised with what confidence we commonly think that natural events are always consistent in their occurrence. To say things happen always in the same way is not true. Careful observation now admits that this is not true. If everything happened exactly the same as it has always happened, there would be no history.

Finally, the idea is sometimes expressed that miracles couldn't be true because science is against them. If scientific observation did not confirm an idea, I did not see how you could ever believe it. But do the miracles actually contradict science? If so, in what do the miracles contradict science? Miracles can occur if you admit that God is able to act spontaneously, if He can do as He pleases. If God can act in His own way—the way in which He wants to act without having to be confined in any way—then there is no scientific rule or principle of law that will bind Him, and He can perform any miracle that is in His will.

CHAPTER 6

Trouble with Miracles

The most stubborn problem I had in the whole matter of placing my full confidence in the Bible was this matter of miracles. These events which were outside the norm of the natural bothered me until I examined my difficulties.

I used to think that the miracle stories were naive embellishments on the part of interested and eager persons who were trying to enhance their stories. But as I studied them I found that those events had aroused wonder among the people who saw them. People found them difficult to believe then, even though the miracle happened before their eyes, and that was the way it was reported. There was no further explanation; that's how it happened. As I kept trying to understand, I thought perhaps the miracles were artful exaggerations on the part of people who wanted to make their story look good. Upon further reflection, it seemed to me that that would be an indictment against the whole text of Scripture; when you think about what is supernatural in the Bible, there is so much that you would be doubting the entire Bible.

At times I found myself just skipping over the miracles. I would read them, but I didn't really come to grips with them, for I always had in mind that possibly this could be disposed of by an explanation in one form or another. I don't think I ever really faced the idea that they were to be accepted as supernatural. Yet, there they were.

I kept thinking about them from time to time, and suddenly it seemed to me that the question of all the miracles hinged on but one—the reality of the resurrection and the ascension. That was what the Bible said a man must believe in order to be saved. If a man believes in his heart that God raised up Jesus Christ from the dead, he will be saved (Romans 10:9). That doesn't leave room for anything else. I tried to understand how a man could believe such things.

I had gone to an average high school in Canada and had taken the usual courses that would be in the curriculum of a North American high school of a generation ago. Without realizing it, I had actually gone through a "brainwashing" with reference to anything outside of the usual run of nature. Scientific axioms had been ground into my mind, and they left me unable to accept the reality or the authenticity of anything that would be different from the normal routine. I was in trouble when I tried to think how a person really could accept the resurrection without some doubt.

My problem was this: I had never seen it happen. In all the cases I knew, men died and stayed dead. I assumed that there could be no change from natural law. When I faced this matter, I asked myself if it could have been possible back in the days when this story was first told that people didn't know about the universality of natural law. Should I think that the hundreds and thousands and now millions of people who have believed this have all been naive? Or had they just believed the story while disregarding the facts? This would mean they had not really accepted it. I then asked: What's the problem? Why can't I believe? What's wrong with it? What am I to believe?

One day during harvest time, I was out in the wheat field and was turning these questions over in my mind. I asked myself: How did I ever get to be here in the first place? Where did I come from? It dawned on me that *creation* is a bigger miracle than *resurrection*. After all if God could make me the first time out of nothing, it wouldn't be so big a problem to make me the second time when He already had me. Maybe that wouldn't impress anybody else, but that particular night when I came in from work I had a strange feeling of relaxation about this whole problem. If I could believe the creation and I was here, why not believe the resurrection? Someone may argue that that didn't prove it to be true. No, it didn't prove it, but it did get my mind loose from a rigid fixation which prejudiced me to think it couldn't be true. When I faced this matter, I was able to admit that if I could be created in the first place, I should be able to be recreated. And suddenly I could believe it. My mental processes were now free to accept the idea.

I tried to understand why I had been so sure it was impossible, and I realized that I had been "brainwashed" on the whole subject of any variation from natural law. I realized that my inability to grasp the idea and give it any kind of credence was due to prejudice—a pre-judgment. I had already settled in my mind and accepted from my high school reading and study that natural law was absolute.

When I went up for my oral examination for my Master's Degree in the university, I was asked, "Where is natural law?" I was fortunate enough to know the right answer: in the mind of the scientist. All the natural laws that were ever made up or heard of are the observed uniformities that occur and which certain men have pointed out. I thought natural law was absolute. In that case there would be no variation and there could be no miracles.

I had also somehow accepted the idea that the universe is impersonal. If there is any power in the universe, it is power such as electricity. If there should happen to be truth in the universe, it is as dead matter in mathematics.

These two ideas—the universe is a dead machine and
natural law is absolute—make it altogether impossible to
believe any miracle. They are really formulated from the
standpoint of philosophy. I had fallen into a form of deism
without being aware of it.

While I was turning these things over in my mind and
feeling in a strange way that I was now loose so that I
could think of the possibility of miracles, I tried to see
how important they were. I purchased a cheap copy of the
New Testament. I checked through it and blotted out every reference to the supernatural or the miraculous in the
Gospels. When I finished, there wasn't much left. Anyone
can do that. Simply get hold of a copy of Scripture, and
every time you come across something that is beyond the
natural, strike it out and see what you have left. It will be
a shocking display.

Through this experiment, I realized several things. In
the first place, if I thought I could believe the Bible but
leave out all things that were supernatural, I might as well
leave the book shut. The whole thing is supernatural. But
more than that, I realized that I needed the miracles to
prepare me in heart and mind to grasp the idea of God's
working. Why, I could barely believe the resurrection with
the mind I had! Where did I get that mind? It came from
the culture and the society in which I lived.

You need some build-up in your mind to prepare you
to believe that God can raise the dead; and if God can't
raise the dead, there is no Gospel. That's the whole point.
The only sign of the Kingdom of God that the Lord Jesus
said would ever be given was the sign of the prophet Jonah.
"For as Jonah was three days and three nights in the
whale's belly; so shall the Son of man be three days and
three nights in the heart of the earth" (Matthew 12:40).
There is no attempt to evade that or to slip it around the
corner. That is straight-out, open, plain, daylight talk. The
Bible presents the fact that God raised Jesus Christ from

the dead. That is all that it does say and there is no way to get away from it. But for me to believe and to accept it, I would need help.

After I was able to grasp the idea of the resurrection, I just had to look up to God. If God was Creator, He could be the Resurrector. No trouble at all. If He could make the world once out of nothing, He surely could make another if He wanted to. That is a very simple and ordinary way of saying that "with God nothing shall be impossible" (Luke 1:37).

Closely related to miracles and to the principle of the supernatural are *demons*. I was very slow to accept the idea of demons. I saw it in the Bible and for that reason I had to believe it. I believed it in a way, but there was always the possibility that the word *demon* was a cultural term used to refer to a certain type of psychic disturbance. That was always possible in my mind, and maybe that was the best language they had in their culture at that time.

I was preparing to be a missionary, but I still didn't believe in demons. I talked with some missionaries who had been on the foreign field, and they gave me their personal testimony of dealing with demons and with people who were demon-possessed. But I doubted those missionaries. I didn't doubt their sincerity and integrity, but I doubted their understanding and intelligence. I decided that they were the kind of people who believed in ghosts.

I thought that perhaps the word *demon* was used in Palestine back in those days because they didn't know about psychological phenomena. I did not face the actual question of whether or not demons really existed. I never added it up until I was a minister. When I was in the university studying psychology as my major, I thought that the whole concept of demons might be a way of referring to something not known in that day. The public then did not know about germs carrying disease. They did not know about psychological states of imbalance.

By that time I was preaching, and I believed that the concept of demons was interlocked with the reality of the devil. If the demons weren't true, then the devil wasn't true. That was linked up with the personality of the Holy Spirit. If the devil isn't a person, then the Holy Spirit is not a person. If the Holy Spirit isn't a person, then angels aren't persons, and if angels aren't persons, then how do we know God is a person? The entire theistic view of God as a person is involved.

When you go on from there, the whole structure of the spiritual world is interlocked. If you doubt the existence of demons, you actually strain the whole conception of the spiritual world. If I had not gotten the matter of demons straightened out, I believe that the whole spiritual structure would have collapsed in my consciousness.

I took a course in personality psychology at the university, and I learned how difficult it is for anyone versed in our culture and using our language to conceive of a person. Psychologists can't tell you what a person is. You may know you're a person and you may know that the members of your family are persons, but no reputable psychologist can give you a simple statement of what that means. If you take some of the experts and professionals along this line and open their books, they might give you a paragraph which, if you could understand it, wouldn't tell you any more than what you started with. I have carried on this discourse at the highest level in my own doctoral program in recent years.

When I sat down and talked things over with my professor of psychology, when I was pursuing my studies toward my Ph.D. degree, he asked me privately, as a Christian, how I could conceive of God as a person. He said that was his big problem, and I remember asking him to tell me what a person is. He relaxed, laughed, and said, "Well, you've got me there." I knew he couldn't tell me psychologically, even though he was a very learned man. I then pointed out to him that if he found it difficult to say what a person is when he was looking at a man, he shouldn't be surprised if he found it difficult to say that God is a person. Sitting across from him there at Columbia University in New York City, I said, "Doctor, you think I'm a person, don't you?" He replied, "Yes." "Well," I said, "I think you are a person." But psychologically we couldn't tell each other what we meant.

When our society has difficulty conceiving of God as a person, it is not surprising it has difficulty conceiving of the Holy Spirit as a person, Satan as a person, angels as persons, and demons as persons.

As I was studying this, I found that the word *soul* does not need to refer to any substance and a *person* need not have any essence. It isn't as though the word *person* implies that there is some mystical kind of thing inside of you that you call "a person." The word *soul* and the word *person* may very well be functional terms by which we refer to certain entities of existence.

One reason we find it difficult to believe in demons as set forth in the New Testament is because demons have personal characteristics and we are not willing to concede that they are persons. For a long time I thought that to believe a demon was a person was to believe that a demon was some sort of little brownie or gremlin. If I believed in demons, I would believe little brown men would stand on my coat collar and whisper things in my ear. But that is purely grotesque imagination.

In our culture we are horrified at the thought of ghosts. Since the word *spirit* means the same thing, we can't think of a spirit without thinking of a ghost. If spirits aren't, then demons aren't. If demons aren't, then Satan isn't. If Satan isn't, then the Holy Spirit isn't, and if the Holy Spirit isn't, then Heaven isn't, hell isn't, God isn't, and we ourselves are just all alone—nobodies in bed in the dark with the blankets pulled up over our heads. That's all. There's nothing outside ourselves.

Why not consider a "person" to be a functional unit—

something that acts and does? Why should I think it has to
have an *avoirdupois* body? Why should I think it has to
have something like arms and legs? My physiological body
has arms and legs; but if I lost my arms or legs I would still
be myself. The "I" in me isn't dependent upon my arms
and legs. It isn't dependent on my body as such. Why
could there not be interpersonal relation between "you"
and "myself" apart from our bodies? Why could a person
not be led by another person? And, if I can be led by another person, then I could be led by the Spirit. If I were
led by the Spirit, I could be driven by Satan. If you will
accept the idea that a man can be spirit-filled, what's your
problem in having him demon-possessed? Who can say it
isn't so? Who knows that much? If the Bible says yes, is it
so? Why not? Who has liberty to refute or deny what the
Bible says?

Since no one can definitely say there aren't demons, and
since the Bible says there are, why not accept it? As for me,
I found I was able to.

I now approach this problem from this angle: I have
satisfactory evidence that God is a person. If God is a person, I am satisfied Jesus Christ is a person, and then I will
accept the Holy Spirit as a person. When I accept the Holy
Spirit to be a person, then I believe the angel Gabriel is a
person. When I think of the angels being persons who can
communicate with human persons, then I will think that
Satan is a person and that Satan's emissaries—his agents,
the demons—are persons.

Thus I was able to free my mind from the negative prejudice and the disposition to say, "No, it can't be true." I
found that it was unnecessary to say it can't be true. So
then, considering the Bible as a whole, I found myself able
to say, I will accept it and say that it is *true,* and go on from
there.

CHAPTER 7

Trouble with Details

I have been talking about having confidence in the Bible, but I am not forgetting that I am not saved through faith in the Bible. *Salvation depends upon believing in Jesus Christ.* I am saved through faith in Him. When I talk about having confidence in the Bible, I mean accepting the Scriptures as the Word of God so that I may study them with the expectation that in them God will set forth certain ideas which He wants me to use as I grow in grace and in knowledge. I can understand more about the Lord Jesus Christ as I have a fuller understanding of what has been set forth in the Scriptures. The Lord Jesus, after His resurrection, opened the understanding of the disciples that they might understand the Scriptures, "And beginning at Moses and all the prophets, he expounded unto them in all the scriptures the things concerning himself" (Luke 24:27). If they needed to understand the Scriptures, I most certainly would profit by that myself.

Should I be able to pick up the Bible with confidence that this material as it is (not as it is changed through criticism and made into something else) is written for my learning, that I "through patience and comfort of the scriptures might have hope" (Romans 15:4)? Is this the way I am to understand it? Am I to understand that "Now all these things happened unto them for examples: and they are written for our admonition, upon whom the ends of the world are come" (1 Corinthians 10:11)? Am I to understand that "All scripture is given by inspiration of God, and is profitable for doctrine, for reproof, for correction, for instruction in righteousness" (II Timothy 3:16)? Am I to stand where Paul stood when he said that he was "believing all things which are written in the law and in the prophets" (Acts 24:14)?

I repeat: my salvation does not depend upon whether or not I believe the Bible to be the Word of God. My salvation depends upon whether or not I believe in Jesus of Nazareth as the Christ, the Son of the living God, and in His death for me. But what I realize very well in this Twentieth Century is that all I know about Jesus of Nazareth is set forth in the Scriptures. Apart from the Word of God written in the Scriptures, I know nothing about Him.

The question I have asked myself repeatedly then is this: how much confidence can I put in the Bible? Can I accept it as the Word of God?

After I became a believer and began studying the Scriptures, I found there were certain problems which seemed to hinder my full confidence in the text.

First there was the *multiplicity of manuscripts*—there was an indefinite number of different manuscripts, and none of them was the original. No one can claim that any particular manuscript is the original. We don't have the notes of the writers of the Psalms. We don't have the original manuscript of the writer of the Book of Job. We don't have the original manuscript of the writer of II Peter. In short, we don't have any originals.

Also, we do not have *one* complete set. We have dozens and probably hundreds of excerpts, fragments, and bits of writings. Are they variant from each other? Yes, in a small way. They are different, but in all these various manuscripts are there any major discrepancies? The answer is: no. Do they contradict each other at any point in which one would say that Christ Jesus died on the cross and another would say He died in bed? Are there any that would say that Israel was in Egypt as a captive nation, slaves, and in another that they never went down to Egypt? No. In telling the story of David slaying Goliath, does any one of them say David killed Goliath by hitting him in the head with a stone and then cutting off his head with a sword, while another relates that he ran a spear through his heart? No. There are no instances of major discrepancies— two statements about the same thing which are entirely contradictory. Differences? Yes. Contradictions? No. The question arises: could you have confidence in such as that?

In more recent years, I have become aware of the discoveries of the papyrus scrolls, certain parchments with a great deal of New Testament material that were written earlier than anything we have in our hands. However, no contradiction of events or change of persons or promises was found—only a corroboration of those things. Even more recently, since World War II, we have all been aroused to a new interest in what has been called the Dead Sea Scrolls. Yet no significant difference from the Old Testament, which we already have, has been seen, but rather much corroboration.

Should the fact that we have these many manuscripts that differ from each other in recording certain minor details cause us to lose confidence in the Bible? One could ask a similar question like this: consider a tune like the National Anthem. It can be pitched in one key and then in another and not have two notes the same in the two scores. The National Anthem may be written for children's voices and also for men's bass voices, and the same notes may not be struck at all, but is it the same tune? Yes. Suppose someone plays the National Anthem and strikes the wrong key. Would it not still be the National Anthem? It certainly would. Suppose also that one played the National Anthem on a piano while another played it on the violin? Would they be different? Yes. Would they be different tunes? No.

Consider the four Gospels in the New Testament. Because there are four Gospels, does it mean that one is right and the other three are wrong? Or do they all say the same thing in the main? Yes. Do they say the same thing in detail? No. Will four eyewitnesses of the same event tell the same story? No. As a matter of fact, if you had four witnesses to a traffic accident and all told the same story, you would have pretty good evidence that someone had organized them. If they came in and told the truth, you would, no doubt, get four different accounts.

With all these different variations there is no change in the *major* details. You will find that Christ Jesus died on Calvary's cross for sinners and you will find He was raised from the dead. There will be no variation in the Gospels. No matter how many ways it is written, no matter how many variations there are in manuscripts, when I read the New Testament there is but one melody that comes through. I read: "Jesus loves me, this I know, for the Bible tells me so." It doesn't matter which version of the Bible you may have; in English they will all be practically the same as far as the actual message is concerned.

In this connection, I bring up another item that gave me some concern for awhile. I wondered whether I should hold off from having full confidence in the Scripture because of the findings of *archaeology*—the diggings in Palestine and Mesopotamia. Would they discover something that would contradict what we already had? They had been doing this digging for a long time. Early in my spiritual experience I heard of Dr. Melvin Grove Kyle, who at that time was considered one of the two or three leading archaeologists of America. He made this statement: "No discovery of archaeology up-to-date in any way discredits any statement in the Bible." I was deeply impressed with that. It is still true. They haven't discovered anything that would discredit one thing in the Bible. They have discovered a great many things which help to confirm it, but I must confess that my confidence is not grounded on that.

When you are studying archaeology, you will probably find the author of your book admitting and pointing out that the whole dating scheme for all that is found in archaeology in Palestine is taken from the Bible. Perhaps we should ask this question, too: would there be any reason to question the soundness and authenticity of Scripture if the inscription on some monuments in old Babylonia contradicted the Bible? Suppose we find some old inscribed stones where something is chiseled out giving a certain record, and we compare it with the records of the same event that are found in the Old Testament, and it turns out that this archaeological discovery differs from what we have in the Old Testament. What shall I think? Should I esteem a comment that had been chiseled into a stone under the direction of some ancient king to be more true than what was written in the manuscript of the Scriptures? After all, if you read the record on a monument found in Assyria telling of a battle being fought and so many soldiers involved, what makes you think they are telling the truth? Would you claim that all military communications today are true? Do you think those numbers aren't padded today when you read about a skirmish that occurred in some far-off battlefield when one side reports there were eighteen dead, and the other side reports there were four dead? Would you really be surprised if both were not correct? Where do we get the notion that this material which is found on these various stones is necessarily absolutely true? Why should we think that they were completely honest if their record should differ from what the Scriptures report?

However, when I checked on archaeology and its findings, as well as the discoveries regarding the various manuscripts, I found many things that increased my confidence in the

Bible, and I came across nothing contrary in any way to what we have in Scripture.

Another problem concerning the validity of Scripture could involve *"the opposition of science."* I have great respect for science. In my own personal career through high school, and afterwards, I was very much impressed with science. I still believe it is very helpful to be scientific about anything. However, a great many things are called scientific which are not scientific; they are only speculative at best.

Science observes what happens and theorizes how things happen, but people using the same language and thus claiming to be scientific start speculating on how things began. Nobody was there, nobody can observe, and how they began is unknown to science. Observers might tell you how things happen now under observation, but they are absolutely unable to tell you on the basis of science how things happened in the beginning.

One of the problems Christians face is the "evolutionary theory." This was not as much a problem to me as you might expect, because before I became a believer I had passed through a stage in which I had accepted Darwinian evolution. I was willing at first to accept Darwin's theory as the likely origin of the species of living things on the face of the earth, but before I came to have faith I gave up on evolution as a likely hypothesis for the simple reason that there was no actual evidence.

The evolutionary theory, as I understood it as a high school student, was this: life began in simple form and then, due to the operation of natural processes, these forms became gradually more complex through some process of natural selection. Due to certain biological urges, differentiation took place so that one species would get to be like this and another would get to be like that. In the survival of the fittest one would outlast the other. You are not supposed to see the actual process because it happens so slowly.

But one thing that bothered me about this theory was that if true, why are there not any elemental forms now? If the more complex form came from the more simple, why didn't they all change? And if you argue that there are simple forms of life that started later, are any starting now? Can anyone give you a single instance where life is starting on its own anywhere in the universe? I never heard of it. By such considerations as that, I gave up on evolution simply because it made claims for which it had no justification within the very scientific perspective it claimed to honor.

I didn't know until recently, when I was helped with this by a friend of mine who had made a study of it, that Darwin himself would not publish his book on "The Origin of Species" simply because he said the case was not proven. There were at least several gaps in the larger argument, and these were so serious that the whole theory simply did not hold together. It was not a proven idea, and he thought it would cause more harm than it would do good. That is what Darwin himself said long, long ago.

My problem, however, was not with evolution, but with the book of Genesis and the story of creation. I was very much impressed by the way in which the story of creation unfolds. When you consider that this material was released probably back in the days when the children of Israel, a small group of people, were existing in the midst of a culture not their own—somewhere in the Near East around Palestine, where they stayed for a long time—isn't it strange that in their account of creation there are no traces of the local stories which the people round about them believed? It is worth thinking about.

Another angle to consider is the matter of our physical science—the way in which we have come to understand so much more about the world as a whole. As you go through the first two chapters of Genesis, can you find any one thing that contradicts a known principle of modern physics? No, you cannot. The researchers in physical science have language for describing what they see, and for the uniformities they observe which the Bible doesn't have. I will take what the Bible has to say. The scientist will take his own technical knowledge and information and skill, and check through the Bible account, and I have yet to hear of a case where a real scientist makes some statement that the Bible contradicts something he knows about nature. I am very much impressed by that.

If you are going to believe the Bible, you will have to believe in another world besides this one—a spiritual world. Is there any reason there shouldn't be a spiritual world? When you are thinking about the other world, remember that the Bible doesn't make it like this one. It is a different world, but the people who are here are going to be there. Is there any real difficulty in believing that? The Bible gives you very little that doesn't depend upon the reality of Heaven and of eternity. We are going to meet God face to face. That is one of the basic ideas in scripture. Is there anyone who knows any reason why that shouldn't be true?

Some people will say blandly that everybody knows the Bible has mistakes in it. I don't. Someone will say everybody knows the Bible contradicts itself. Not everybody. I am one of the "everybody" and I don't know that it contradicts itself. Differences? Yes. I am *different* from every man I meet, but that doesn't mean I *contradict* every man I meet. And being satisfied in mind and heart that the Bible is trustworthy brings assurance of faith. I know this because that is what it has done for me.

CHAPTER 8

Strength for Today

Not only do I believe in God and the Gospel and in all the things the Bible teaches, but I feel sure about those things which I believe, those things to which I now commit myself. Because the Bible presents them and I feel sure about them, this gives me peace in my mind and heart. I have peace about God. The Bible is full of evidence concerning His justice and His mercy and His truth. As I read the Bible, I am impressed with how reliable God is, how trustworthy He is, and it gives me peace of mind and heart to think that He is my God.

I also have peace about the Lord Jesus Christ. Whenever I read in the New Testament and the Gospels how the Scriptures were fulfilled in His life and in His public ministry, I have an increasing confidence in Him, and that gives me peace about the things that are told about Him. So much of His career is supported by that which went before. When I read about the miracles, I realize they are amazing and wonderful, and I can consider them in various ways. I am persuaded that they are true, and I know that the miracles reported in the New Testament are like the miracles that were reported in the Old Testament. I know that in the Old Testament the promise was made that when the Messiah came He would do these miracles. The understanding was, according to the prophets, that when Christ came He would act in a certain way. Then I read that that is the way He did act. All this has a confirming effect in my mind, and I find myself more and more at peace about the things that are said about the Lord Jesus Christ. It is kind of peace that comes to you when you have no question in your mind.

I have confidence with reference to the Holy Spirit. Ordinarily, the way people talk about the Holy Spirit, I might imagine that this is a figure of speech. I might think that this is a way of speaking nicely about the disposition to do the will of God and that by "the Holy Spirit" is meant the frame of mind of believers or something of that nature. But when I read in the Bible, I find that it sets forth the Holy Spirit as a person. I find that the Holy Spirit is referred to in the Old and New Testaments—all through the Bible—as actually one of the Godhead. The Holy Spirit as a person is One who had certain things to do and did them. He is the One who selects and directs those who are to serve and makes their service effectual. I read these things in the Bible, and they give me more and more confidence that the Holy Spirit will actually affect me and use me. They give me a certain quietness and assurance. The Holy Spirit is no mere figure of speech, because the Bible sets Him forth as a person.

When I look around me, I can't see God nor can I see the Holy Spirit. I could understand what people say about Him, but maybe that would be true and maybe it would not. It could be just a manner of speaking. But when I read about it in the Scriptures, something more tangible is put into my consciousness, something more concrete is put into my thinking, and I am more at peace about Him.

Consider now the matter of forgiveness. I realize that it is a wonderful thing to be forgiven, and I cherish in my memory the freedom of my spirit and the joy that came to me when I felt sure that God had forgiven me. When I read in the Bible, I find that forgiveness is God's way. He has forgiven many people and He is ready to forgive anybody. When I see some of the people in the Scriptures who were forgiven—how they came to the Lord, and how He graciously forgave them—my confidence in forgiveness is confirmed. This is the plan of God. Even though I feel in myself that forgiveness is wonderful and I could wonder in myself whether I could ever be forgiven, for I know I am not worthy, yet I have confidence because the Bible teaches it so clearly and I have confidence in the Bible.

The same would be true with reference to the providence of God. As I live along day in and day out, I depend a great deal on the providence of God. I have a certain quietness and peace because I have an inward assurance that all things are in His hands. This is not just something that has come to me because I could see the hand of God in my affairs. From what I read in the Bible I can see how many different people, who at one time or another were in fear and trembling about certain things, found that "He hath done all things well" (Mark 7:37). When this comes to my mind, I have an increased, confirmed, and grounded confidence in God with reference to His providence, and that gives me a peace about it.

I can read the Psalms, see how their writers would on occasion be distressed and disturbed, and how they would then trust in the providence of God. I remember such passages as "I had fainted, unless I had believed to see the goodness of the Lord in the land of the living" (Psalms 27: 13). But the psalmist *saw* the goodness of the Lord in the land of the living, and that is why he didn't faint.

There are many similar passages in the Scriptures describing people who lived in relationship with God wherein they trusted Him, put their confidence in Him, saw His hand upon them in their affairs for good. For instance, look at the case of Joseph. His brothers sold him as a prisoner and he was made a slave. He was mistreated, abused, lied about and put into prison; but God brought him out to be the ruler of Egypt. Next to the Pharaoh, he was the top man in the entire country. When his brothers afterwards wanted to make sure he would not repay them for the evil that they had done, he said to them, "Ye thought evil against me; but God meant it unto good . . . to save much people alive" (Genesis 50:20). I see in the life of Joseph a remarkable exhibition of the providence of God. By allowing things to happen the way in which they did, He brought Joseph into a place where he actually helped people. That encourages me to believe "that all things work together for good to them that love God, to them who are the called according to his purpose" (Romans 8:28).

Having confidence in the Bible gives me a certain quietness and confidence about my own experience in providence. I find that I am actually able to rest at peace with reference to tomorrow. "Sufficient unto the day is the evil thereof" (Matthew 6:34). The Bible sets forth that obviously God will prevail. He has His hand upon my affairs and He will bring His will to pass. "He will not fail nor be discouraged." These various passages of Scripture come to my mind, and I know in the hand of God I can be safe.

With reference to the world, the Bible teaches me that God made the world. "In the beginning God created the heaven and the earth" (Genesis 1:1). He made the world as it is and He overrules and controls it. He holds the world in His hands so that the nature and the purpose of the world is under control. I'll take the world as it is, for I am not going to stay here anyway. I'll live in the world and know that God is able to overrule and do all things well.

As I look around me and see the evil which seems to run riot at times, I don't see how many men can escape the world's crashing in on them like a flood, like the waves of the ocean; but I remember that the Bible presents God as on the throne. He is overruling all things and He can make the wrath of man to praise Him. I get the feeling from the Bible that evil is like the waves of the ocean—they will come just as far and no farther. God has set the bounds of the ocean and the bounds of the rage of men, and He won't let either go any farther than the limit which He has set.

If anyone were to ask me, "Now that you have confidence in the Bible, what difference does it make?" I would point out it makes this difference: that in the assurance I have in my faith, I find a great peace about everything, and from that peace comes strength. Because of the Bible as it is, I have strength to persist with what I am doing and to endure any kind of circumstances and experiences.

When trouble comes, the Bible will tell me that God overrules all things. When trouble comes the Bible tells me, "Yet man is born unto trouble, as the sparks fly upward" (Job 5:7). The Bible tells me how the Lord Jesus Christ said, "In the world ye shall have tribulation: but be of good cheer; I have overcome the world" (John 16:33). Trouble is unpleasant, I know, and it can upset and disturb and bother us; it can hurt us, but we have strength to go through with it. Why? Because the Bible gives us so much evidence of the fact that God is able to overrule and to make even the wrath of man to praise Him.

So also with the confusion that is round about us. Undoubtedly the confusion in the world is distressing and disturbing. People are frightened, upset, and discouraged by it; but I find the Bible gives me a certain strength even in my confusion. My strength is in my confidence that God is not confused. How did I find that out? From the Scriptures. I see various types of confusion and turmoil referred to in the Bible, but none of it is with God. He is strong. He is over all. He knows what He is doing, and if in that connection I think to myself that there are so many things I don't know, the Bible tells me, "The secret things belong unto the Lord our God: but those things which are revealed belong unto us and to our children for ever" (Deuteronomy 29:29). Because these statements are there and because they speak to my situation, I am encouraged to believe that the other things are true. In my confusion I go on steadfastly, not because I am strong and not because I am determined and dogged in my attitude, but because I am expectant. I am really expecting that God will come through.

Someone may say that is just faith in God. I know it is faith in God, but don't say *just* faith in God. *It is faith in God grounded in the Scriptures.* The Bible strengthens my confidence in Him because it illustrates His way of doing things. In the times of my failure, when the things I have done are not what they ought to be, I have strength to go on because the Bible tells me that God can overrule. I can think of people named in the Scriptures who did not do what they should have done, but God overruled; and because they turned to Him, He was able to control. The instances related in the Scriptures and the promises found there combine to give me a strength to persist and to endure in the face of any discouraging circumstances.

The very fact that I hold the Bible to be the Word of God and I look upon it as a reliable source of revelation from Him gives me a certain joy in my daily experience. Day by day as I go along believing in the Lord and having confidence in Him, I have a blessed assurance. This assurance brings me an inward blessing because it is so clearly confirmed. I feel so sure about all things. At times I am in a situation where I would be tempted to do something rash or impulsive, and the Scriptures speak to quiet me. They speak caution. They say, "Wait on the Lord: be of good courage, and he shall strengthen thine heart" (Psalm 27: 14). I have joy in my victories, and this joy is increased because of the confidence, the assurance that I have.

In looking forward to tomorrow, I actually expect things will be better. I expect things to work out in a way that will glorify God because I know He is a living Being and the Scriptures reveal that there is no end to His grace or mercy. He is always wanting to do something on behalf of those who put their trust in Him. When I trust Him and when you trust Him, we can expect that tomorrow will bring victories, for this is the promise of God.

Believing the Bible to be reliable, I accept what it says. If I want to understand about the world, I read in the Bible. If I want to understand about history, I look in the Scriptures. I find in the Bible a revelation of the hand of God upon the affairs of men, and because of that I have a certain understanding in my outlook. When I look at anything, I have ideas which I get from the Bible that help me to evaluate that situation.

For instance, I have an understanding about the universe because of what the Bible says. When I consider the world and everything in it, whether thinking about space, the sun, moon, and stars, or the things that are found round about me, I understand all this in relation to the Bible. God made the universe, and when He looked at it He said, "It was very good" (Genesis 1:31). I am persuaded that it is, and because of that I have a certain quietness and a certain confidence about it. I feel that all things are under His control, and they are being moved toward a glorious climax because God's hand is upon them.

When I look at the reports in the newspapers, read the problems in the magazines, consider what people are thinking all over the world, so that I have the affairs of the world in mind, I also have the Bible in my hand. I read what the Bible has to say. It helps me understand the affairs of the world. Over all the turmoil in the nation God is on the throne. The nations themselves are like the waves of the sea. They are driven by the wind and tossed. But the Bible says that God on the throne overlooks all things and that He has His hand upon all affairs.

If you have the Bible in your mind and heart, you will understand that God "hath made of one blood all nations of men for to dwell on all the face of the earth, and hath determined the times before appointed, and the bounds of their habitation" (Acts 17:26). With that in mind you will feel differently about current affairs among men.

So when someone asks me, "Don't you think there is a possibility that a certain nation will wipe out everything?" My answer is: "No!" "What makes you think that? Do you see anything to oppose them?" "No," I will say. They then ask, "Why do you feel that way?" My answer is: "God will overrule." "What makes you say that?" "The Bible says so."

If any will protest that not everybody is satisfied with that, I admit humbly I am not speaking for everybody; I am giving my testimony. With these things in mind there is a certain understanding of the affairs of the world. The same is true with people. When you think about wicked people and their schemes and the way they are going, considering the Bible will help you to understand these things. You understand that such people are in darkness: they are like sheep scattered without a shepherd, and the turmoil and confusion they have is in their hearts.

Because of the Bible, I am satisfied that I was born where I was to be born and had the appearance I was to have and that God Himself overruled all things. Is that because I see His hand in my daily affairs? Can I almost feel that what I am doing at any moment is something that the Lord wants me to do" No. My comment is on the whole outline; the whole scope of my life, my experience and my affairs are in relation to God. I really believe God has His hand on me, as He has His hand on you. I understand that is the way it is. This makes me think God overruled all things in my childhood. God has overruled all the things in my life up to this day, and everything that happens to me now happens by the grace of God. The understanding which I have of this I receive from the Scriptures.

Finally, I believe in another world; I believe in a spirit-

ual reality. I think that a number of very important things
are real because the Bible says they are real. I think I have
a soul. I can't see it, and I understand all the things that
the psychologists say one way or another about it that
would dismiss the idea. And yet I think I have a soul.
Why? Because the Bible talks about it. I have confidence
in the Bible. I believe also in the reality of God, the judgment of God, the overruling providence of God, the hand
of God in human affairs, and the fact that God is the Judge
of all the earth and every man will come face to face with
Him. Those things are very real in my consciousness because the Bible speaks of them.

I believe these things, not because they look good to me,
nor because I can see what they imply and how they fit. I
believe these things because I get them from scripture.

When you have confidence in the Bible and you have the
Bible in your hand, you will believe you have a soul, you
will believe that God is in Heaven, that He is the Judge,
and you will believe there is such a thing as sin. I do. I
think that sin is the particular quality of *human* conduct
that God sees. I sin when anything I do is not as God
would have me do it. God is the Judge, and that makes sin
a reality. Because of sin, souls will die. "For the wages of
sin is death" (Romans 6:23). I believe that. I have it in my
heart and mind because it is in the Bible. I derived it from
the Bible.

The same is true with reference to the Gospel. I believe
a sinner can be saved. I believe that "Though your sins be
as scarlet, they shall be as white as snow; though they be
red like crimson, they shall be as wool" (Isaiah 1:18). I
believe it because it is in the Bible, and I have confidence
in the Bible. The marvelous truth that "God receiveth sin-
ful men" is expressed all the way through the Bible.

I think the Holy Spirit is a real person, and He will come
to you and to me if we put our trust in the Lord Jesus
Christ. God will send Him. This means that no Christian

person needs to walk alone, because he will have the Holy Spirit as his divine Companion. My reason for thinking this is that this is what the Bible says.

Because I believe the Bible to be true, because I take the Bible as a reliable, authentic revelation of the will of God, I believe in prayer. I believe in prayer not because I have had so many answers to prayer, although I *have* had answers by the grace of God. I believe in prayer not because *I can* absolutely guarantee that if you ask in a certain way certain results will follow. I believe in prayer because men in the Bible prayed and God heard them. I go by the Scriptures and the Scriptures speak to my heart. Because I have the Bible in my hand and I have confidence that it is reliable, as I read that God will answer prayer I believe it. I read in the Bible, "Ask, and it shall be given you; seek, and ye shall find; knock, and it shall be opened unto you" (Matthew 7:7). I believe those promises because they are in the Bible.

I believe in Heaven. I have never been there; I have never seen it; I have never seen anyone come back from Heaven, but the Bible speaks about it, and because the Bible speaks about it, I believe it. In the same way, I believe the devil is real. I know there are people who don't believe it, but I do. There is no question about it in my mind at all. I depend upon the Bible and I take this to be true.

Furthermore, I receive help from the Bible in daily living. When I go by what I find in the Bible, I feel that I am acting in the will of God. If I have trouble, the Bible has promises which come to my heart and I will find myself comforted. I get strength for my daily confidence. If I want to turn to God at any time, I open the Bible and read it and I have a blessing in my soul. My reason for opening the Bible is that I have confidence in it—it is the revelation of God.

Therefore, in all these various ways, because I believe

the Bible to be true, much good comes to me in the way of peace, assurance, confidence, guidance and understanding.

Remember as you read this, I am simply saying that this is what I know to be true in my own experience. I am persuaded God is no respecter of persons. I do not think I am receiving any special or unusual treatment. I am sure anyone who looks where I look will see what I see. As I go on living among my fellow men and sharing with many, I am more and more concerned that all should hear the witness of the heart that trusts the Bible: "Great peace have they that love thy law: and nothing shall offend them" (Psalm 119:165).

CHAPTER 9

Facing Criticism

I know there are people who feel they cannot take the Scriptures at their face value. Some people will even say they trust the Bible, while they do not really believe what it says.

Some people will tell you the Bible is the Word of God, but they do not believe the miracles. They will tell you they believe the Bible is the Word of God, but they do not believe there is a devil or a hell. They will tell you they believe the Bible is the Word of God, but they do not believe the literal resurrection from the dead. Such inconsistency creates confusion for everyone.

Some folks have the idea that educated people are not so likely to believe all the Bible. This is very common. In fact I have found that when a man begins to disbelieve, he is often spoken of as being "progressive." The skeptical attitude toward the Bible is generally called "advanced thinking." Here it may help to remember that you can advance out as well as you can advance in. There are those who would say that any person is naive who believes the Bible. They will say he is not realistic.

The popular feeling seems to be that the Scriptures are not really reliable. How do we face this? When we hear criticism and objections to the Scriptures, we will remember that when the Lord Jesus Christ was here on earth, He, too, was criticized. He lived openly in this world; He talked openly, and He performed His miracles in full view of all the people; but the world did not receive Him. "He came unto his own, and his own received him not" (John 1:11). John says, ". . . the world knoweth us not, because it knew him not" (1 John 3:1). The world did not admit the reality of these spiritual things shown by the Lord, and in the same way the world does not know nor does it respect and esteem the Bible.

I am reminded of that incident in the Gospel of John, telling of the man who was born blind. When the Lord Jesus met him He performed a miracle and opened the man's eyes.

The Pharisees came to the man and asked, "Who opened your eyes?" The man replied, "I don't know. A man that is called Jesus came and did it." Then the Pharisees told him that whoever did it was not a good man because the man who opened his eyes was a Sabbath-breaker; therefore, he was an evil man. The blind man answered: "Whether he be a sinner or no, I know not: one thing I know, that, whereas I was blind, now I see" (John 9:1–25).

This is, after all, the testimony against which all arguments, insinuations, questions, and criticisms fall to the ground. The person who has actually been cured by the medicine is the person who can bear testimony that the medicine is effectual, regardless of opinions held by such as never took the medicine.

Opposition to God is to be found all over the world. We all know that everybody doesn't believe in God or trust in God. Everybody doesn't receive the Lord Jesus Christ or follow the Gospel. This is bound to eventuate in attacks on the Bible. The Lord was often questioned and many times slandered. No wonder the Bible is subject to the same kind of abuse. Believers are often questioned and are oftentimes

slandered. It is not a surprising thing that the Bible should
be also.

When I come up against criticism and skepticism about
the Bible, I try to recall what the grounds of my confidence
in the Bible are. Do I believe in the Bible because I know
it is accurate? Do I believe in the Bible because I know its
promises are true? Or, do I believe in the Bible because it
is effectual, because it actually works?

My first confidence in the Bible was grounded in the
testimony of Christianity. The witness of Christianity in
centuries of history gave me a tremendous predisposition
to think the Bible must be trustworthy. That was impressive enough, but then there was also the personal testimony
of the people who believed. Believing people, who claim
they believe the Bible, will testify that they took this medicine and that it cured them. This I did myself. In reading
and studying the Bible I came to the point where I accepted its message; I committed myself to it, and it affected
me.

Add all that up. Why do I have confidence in the Bible?
I have confidence in the Bible because of its effectiveness,
because of its function, and because of its performance. In
other words, I have confidence in the truth of it because
the truth actually makes the difference. "And ye shall know
the truth, and the truth shall make you free" (John 8:32).
Because I have confidence in the truth of this and its effectiveness, it predisposes me to have confidence in its de-
pendability, and that moves on to where I have confidence
in its accuracy.

It would be very hard for me to think as a logical person
that a book which promotes morals is in itself a lie. Am I
to understand that the book which is associated with virtue
is an evil book? No, that doesn't make sense. My confidence
in the Bible is grounded in its effectual function. It wasn't
the accuracy of the Bible that brought me to faith. I came
to believe the Bible because believing it, receiving it in the

heart, and yielding myself to it effected the results which
it had promised. Whenever anyone brings out any criticism
of the Bible, I try to bring him back to the ground on
which I came to believe. Anything I now have to say about
the Bible will not be a matter of answering the criticism
or convincing the critic, but it will be witnessing to my own
faith.

Someone may say that you must examine the language,
the grammar, the structure, and the historicity of the Bible.
I ask, "Who says so?" Paul reminded Timothy, "But continue thou in the things which thou hast learned and hast
been assured of, knowing of whom thou hast learned them"
(II Timothy 3:14). I think it is very, very important when
you are challenged to open your mind to an idea to ask
who is giving the idea.

If someone is going to teach me, I want to know something of the man who is doing the teaching. Suppose someone tells me that this man is a great scholar. I don't know
exactly what makes a great scholar, but let me examine
such a claim.

Did great scholars recognize Jesus? The scholars in the
time of the Lord Jesus Christ were called scribes. Did they
recognize Christ? It is astonishing and sobering that the
scribes and Pharisees in Jerusalem didn't know Him. Why
would this present-day scholar know? Has it been the great
scholars throughout history who have presented Jesus
Christ? With some brilliant exceptions the opposite has too
often been tragically true.

Did a great scholar win me to Jesus Christ? Were there
not some intelligent and educated people in Manitoba,
Canada, where I grew up as a young man? Did any of those
educated people win me? The answer is, "No, they didn't
win me." I don't know whether they talked about the Bible
or not. It is possible they did. Some of them were preachers, but they never took one step in my direction. If they
took no steps to win me, why should I now let them take

any steps to confuse me? Why should I pay attention to
their questions? They never spoke to me before; why do
they come to examine me now? They did *nothing* about
my unbelief. They didn't come to show me that my unbelief was wrong. Why should I let such a man lead me now
when he didn't lead me before? The men who came to deal
with me were humble men, simple men. It was they who
believed the Bible.

It is proposed again that everybody (the majority)
agrees with the conclusion of the critic. Oh, no! I happen
to know that much myself. Even if the majority did agree,
would that be valid? If I were the only witness who was to
testify to my faith on earth, would that make any difference?

If I put my hand in water and I find it to be cold, do I
have to wait on ten scientists to tell me it is cold? I know
it's cold. If I have believed in the Scriptures and they have
spoken peace to my heart, do I need fourteen psychologists
to explain it to me? They didn't help me get it: why should
I let them take it away from me?

Someone will say that I'm not answering the questions.
They are right. I didn't raise their questions, and I don't
answer their questions. I don't intend to try to answer their
questions. You may then say, "Do you feel confident about
your procedure?" I do. "On what grounds?" Very humbly
I would point you to the Gospels. Read Matthew, Mark,
Luke and John. The Lord Jesus was asked questions on
every hand. They bombarded Him with questions. Read
through the Gospels and find out how the Lord Jesus answered His questioners. He seldom ever answered a question on the ground it was asked. Such questions were often
asked in unbelief and ignorance, and our Lord never took
the position of unbelief or ignorance to answer them.

I came to have confidence in the Bible on the ground
of a simple, personal need which the Bible supplied. I had

a great inward empty feeling in my soul, and that emptiness was actually ruining me. Other people have had the same. I found that Christianity represented something I could wish I had. The Bible was at the center of it. Individual believers testified to something I wished I had. The Bible was what they had. I myself came to something that satisfied my soul. It was based upon receiving the Scriptures, and I had the Scriptures in my hand.

Now certain people come with their questions, and they want to question the Bible. On what ground? Their ground. Not I! Let them come on my ground! Come to me and show me the Bible doesn't affect me. Go to these various believers whose testimonies are known to the world and tell them that they are wrong. Rewrite history and show that Christianity is due to something other than the import of the Scriptures. You do that; then I'll listen to you.

Someone may possibly say that an approach like that will not win the college folks. How do you know? In the first place, let me tell you something: it often does. But suppose it didn't win the college folks. Would that make the criticism valid? Would it make my approach wrong? Did the Apostle Paul win all people? Was he wrong? Did the early apostles win all people? Were they wrong? Did the Lord Jesus Christ win all people? Was He wrong? Did Moses convert Pharaoh? Was he wrong? Did the Lord Jesus convert Pilate? Was He wrong? If my procedure doesn't convert anybody, does that alone make me wrong?

When I am asked how I meet criticism, I answer that I meet it mostly by evading it. They have no right to criticize. They are interfering with my personal experience in faith. They didn't give me the faith, but now they want to take it away. Someone will say that I am just protecting myself because I am afraid. Yes, I am protecting myself. I protect myself the way I do when I drive a car in traffic. I protect myself just the way I do when I am inoculated against a disease. I protect myself and have no hesitation about it at all. I try to avoid pitfalls; I try to avoid disease; I try to avoid calamity.

Someone will further argue that if my faith was strong enough I would be able to face criticism of the Bible and the Gospel. I do not have any special concern about what is going to happen to my faith, but I am thinking about what will happen to my time as well as to my peace of mind. I am actually thinking about what will honor my Lord.

That is the way I think about the Bible. Someone will say that I seem to be pretty sure of myself. No, I am not that sure of myself; I am sure of the Lord. I am sure of the Bible. I am sure of the Bible because it is the medicine that cured me. If someone comes along and tells me to put something else in the medicine, I say, "No, you don't put anything else into it; leave the medicine as it is." Someone else says, "Let's process it and take some of the things out of it." No, you don't take anything out of it; leave it as it is because this is the formula that effected a cure in me.

When anyone says that I seem to be confident of myself, all I can say is that this is the way in which I came to faith. This is what now gives me the quietness and peace of mind which I have. Yes, I am sure of that, but I am not sure of myself. I am confident in the Lord Jesus Christ, and I am going to stay with Him.

Can I ignore all the questions? Yes, I can. Should I attempt to answer them? Why should I? A great many people with all their goodwill and their very generous dispositions are entering into the argument and seeking to answer these questions, and not only do they waste time, but they can leave wrong impressions. Suppose I undertook to answer all the questions and I couldn't answer them, what impression would I make on other people? They would say, "He believes in something he can't even explain." This would be the truth, and the foolish thing would be that I should ever have let myself try to explain everything.

How can I have confidence in the Bible when so many people do not believe as I do? How could Paul believe in the Lord when all the other Pharisees of his time didn't believe? How could Peter believe in the Lord when so many hundreds of people didn't believe? How could that small company of disciples believe in the Lord when thousands of people agreed to put Him to death? Besides, I am by no means the only person who believes. Mention Paul, add all the apostles, add all the great servants of God throughout history, bring in all the great missionaries, and bring in the great evangelists. If you were to line up all the people who believe the Bible as the Word of God, you would be surprised at the company I am in.

Do I have any support for my view of ignoring these questions and stiff-arming, shoving them aside? Yes, I certainly do. The New Testament uses the Old Testament Scriptures with total confidence. The writers raised no questions about them. They quoted them as the Word of God. They gave what today would be called an "uncritical acceptance." Why should I do differently?

The question may be raised as to whether or not I think we have made progress since the New Testament time? Progress toward better understanding? Let us suppose, for the sake of argument, that we are going to make a claim that *we have better understanding than people used to have*. In that case *there should be better results*. If criticism *refines* the Bible to discover the *pure* Word of God, then the results of the critic should be strong. They should be more powerful and more effectual. Do you find these critics better evangelists, better missionaries, and better believers? I think the answer is obvious.

I came to have confidence in the Bible because of its functional effectiveness in the world, seen in Christianity.

I came to have confidence in the Bible because of its functional effectiveness in individual people, seen in the personal witness of the believer. My confidence was confirmed and strengthened in the functional effectiveness of the message of the Bible in my own personal experience. That is the ground of my confidence. If anybody is going to come asking questions, let him come down to that level and ask the questions at that point. I'll be right at home to meet him there.

I did not come to believe in the Bible because I knew all the Hebrew and the Greek. I didn't come to believe in the Bible because I knew all the history of the surrounding nations and could prove to you that the historical items in the Scriptures were supported by archaeological discoveries and certain historical research. I have been able to establish many of these as matters of history, but that is not how I came to believe.

From my point of view, I bring all the criticism down to the level of where I stood when I accepted the Gospel, and I find that ground cannot be shaken. If men cannot shake that, I pay no attention to the criticism. This is my attitude towards meeting criticism of the Bible as being reliably the revelation of God's will.

CHAPTER 10

Evaluating Testimony

How could a man gain confidence in the Bible? Even if one did not believe the Bible to be the revelation of God, the claims which are made for the Bible by Christians are enough to attract sincere attention.

All men share one thing in common—living in the world with all of its problems. All are continually confronted by situations in which they are not strong enough, wise enough, or good enough to do what the situation requires. Many men admit they need help, quite apart from the Bible. Some will claim or will seek help through religion, and they will hope that in some way they might be strengthened for what the days before them hold. Some people will specifically seek for help through the Christian Gospel.

The Bible has been in the world for centuries. People have made claims of benefits derived from the Bible for hundreds of years: wherever Christians have gone this book has been taken along, and they have indicated that the Bible is the source of the help that they receive.

Suppose a man is sick with a seemingly incurable illness. He is at the point where he will consider any medicine which might possibly rid him of the disease. Even though he doesn't have all confidence in a particular type of treatment, if other people claimed that that treatment is useful and successful, he can't help but be interested in it. No apology is needed for anyone to take a look at the Bible. We are in enough trouble as human beings, and if there is any help available we would like to have it. When we have believers say to us that that help is available in the Bible, it would be a proper thing to look at it. In fact, a refusal to look at the Bible, considering the claims that are made for it, would plainly smack of prejudice. A man would have to be definitely prejudiced against the Bible not to take a real, sincere look at it in view of his needs on the one hand and the claims of the believers on the other.

When we look at the Bible from the point of view of a man who has no confidence in it but merely considers it a book that Christians have, we can tell this man that the Bible presents two major themes.

There are the Ten Commandments as a code for conduct. Anybody considering the Bible does not go far before thinking about the Ten Commandments and their moral implications seem self-evident. The Bible states, "Thou shalt not kill" (Exodus 20:13). I cannot think of anybody in the world, of any culture whatever, who is going to say that it is all right to kill somebody. The Bible says, "Thou shalt not steal" (Exodus 20:15). Men everywhere think stealing is wrong because they do it at night, in order not to be seen.

You could go down the list and discover that the Ten Commandments are actually a verbalized formalized outward statement of what the conscience of man, according to Paul in Romans, would sustain all the way through. "For when the Gentiles, which have not the law, do by nature the things contained in the law, these, having not the law, are a law unto themselves: which show the work of the law written in their hearts, their conscience also bearing witness, and their thoughts the meanwhile accusing or else excusing one another" (Romans 2:14–15).

The Bible presents the Ten Commandments as a code for conduct. People may not obey this code; but generally speaking they will say that if anyone is going to do what is right and good, he will have to act along the line of the Ten Commandments. The Ten Commandments have elements in them that some people may not understand, but men will generally concede that the Commandments are right as far as they understand them.

The other major theme throughout the Bible is that a sinner can be saved. The salvation of sinners through Jesus Christ includes such ideas as the healing of that which is sick and diseased; the conversion of that which is rebellious and alienated; the change of heart in a person who has been opposed to God; the regeneration of a life that has been dead, being born again in a new way before God; the Holy Spirit coming into the hearts of men; and Heaven itself. If anybody were to present the idea that Jesus Christ will just improve things for you in this world, he would not be presenting the Scriptures.

So, when you are wondering whether or not you will believe the Bible, bear in mind these two major themes: the Ten Commandments as a code for moral conduct; and salvation through Jesus Christ by the power of God, by which a sinner can be saved from his own sin and guilt, and regenerated as a new creature who will be minded to obey God.

The fact that there are various manuscripts of Biblical material is not really significant to the man on the outside, because all these manuscripts are not significantly different. Anything I can tell you that is in the Gospel of the Lord Jesus Christ is in any of the manuscripts. The obscure origin of the manuscripts should be no real handicap because the Bible presents itself as a functional item. It presents itself as being able to do something for you. As such, it is to be judged on its effectiveness. A man who is sick merely asks that the medicine work. This is the way in which a man can approach the Bible to find out whether or not it is really dependable.

All human beings, no matter where you find them in the world, are afflicted with fear of the unknown (fear of the unknown in the universe and fear of the unknown in the future). It is a wonderful thing to be assured that everything is in the hands of a gracious God.

A second common condition of man is a certain bondage within himself. Men sometimes are in bondage to inner habits. They cannot do the things they want to do because of the habits they have developed. They can be in bondage to certain ideas, ideas that they have accepted from the community in which they live and belong; and they may be in bondage to certain relationships. They have to act according to the society of which they are a part. These habits, these ideas, these relationships which men have prevent liberty of action.

One further condition that troubles any man is weakness. Human beings feel their own weakness and limitations, and it scares them. Human beings have weakness even when deciding to do what they know to be right, and certainly they have weakness which leaves them unable to bear the unavoidable burdens, distresses, miseries, and sufferings of life as it is lived in this world. It works out something like this: as a human being with the capacity to appreciate good, I am personally evil; with insight to know what is right, I personally persist in doing wrong; with a sense of justice that would condemn evil wherever it is to be found, I myself am guilty of doing evil; with a nature that needs fellowship, I am alone in the inner recesses of my own soul. This is the general state of men's sickness, and it caused the Apostle Paul to say, "O wretched man that I am" (Romans 7:24)!

Does the Bible offer to help? The answer is *yes*. Simply, plainly, unequivocally: yes. The Bible offers no formula for personal success; it will not make a big man out of me. It offers no formula for financial success; it will not make a rich man out of me. It offers no formula for social success; it will not make a prominent man out of me. But the Bible promises me forgiveness that will take away fear, cleansing that will take away my bondage, and deliverance that will take away my weakness and the limitations I experience because of it. The Bible promises me peace in my heart, comfort for my spirit, joy in my soul, and strength for my life. The Bible promises me everything I need. All things that pertain to life and godliness are revealed in and promised by the Bible.

How will the Bible help? The Bible helps by bringing me to God. As I receive the message of the Bible as valid and believe in its guidance by my obedience, I will be reconciled to God who can and will save me. I am to take the Bible like medicine. I am to *receive it* into my being and *believe it* to be true, and these things will follow.

If I had no previous experience with the Bible, and were without confidence in it, would there be any considerations that I could raise that would predispose me to believe in it? If you meet a man who has no confidence at all in the Bible and you tell him to believe it, he can't. But on what grounds could he believe it? How can a man gain confidence in the Bible? And here again, the Bible is to be taken something like medicine. How can I have confidence in medicine which I have never taken and which no one else I know has ever taken? Why shouldn't I think it might poison me? How can I gain confidence in a doctor to whom I have never gone? How will I get confidence in a garage repair shop where I am going to take my car? How will I gain confidence in a bridge over which I have never travelled?

There is a fairly clear pattern which a man can follow about any of these things. In the first place, a person could pay attention to the public reports. What do men say about this doctor? What do they say about this garage? What do the travelers say about this bridge? What do other patients say about this medicine? Is this not a valid way of acquiring confidence when I am not equipped to do specialized research myself? How about former customers? Are they satisfied customers?

What do men say about the Bible? Do not pay too much attention to what the man who doesn't believe the Bible says about it, because he doesn't take the medicine. Let us turn to the man who has taken the Scriptures and believes in them. Do we know any former customers who have actually depended on the Bible? Are there any satisfied customers who have taken the Bible into their hearts and been blessed? That would be the first general step. Look around and ask who knows anything about this and listen to what he has to say.

In the second place, notice the public results. Don't go just by what the man says. Don't go just by what Christian people say. Look around in society: has the Bible had any affect upon people?

Think again of the illustration of a medicine. Do you believe that inoculation for diphtheria is any good? Do you think that vaccination for smallpox is any good? Would you have confidence in vaccine for polio? Let me ask you about the facts. What has happened to diphtheria? What has happened to smallpox? What is being done regarding polio? From these facts, wouldn't you have good grounds for having confidence in the vaccine?

Now look at the Bible. Consider the mass testimony of Christianity. Christians will tell you that it is God's Word. They will say to you that it is a good book. For you or me to stand back and say, "I don't believe," is not to say anything special about the Bible. Skeptics don't know anything about the Bible. They are not passing any judgment on the Bible, for they don't know what is in it. They are saying that the testimony of the whole world is all wrong.

They are saying that all the Christians whose testimony we hear are fools and crooks. Can anyone say that and have good sense? I don't think so.

The third step I would suggest is that you listen to the witness of believers. Look more closely into what the individual says who actually uses the Bible. Listen to the personal testimony of those who do believe it and notice the character of these witnesses. If one of them says such a thing as, "Once I was blind, now I see," is the man a liar? Why should you call him a liar? Why should he be mistaken? Why should you call him a fool? Why not let the truth come out just as he says it? "I took this medicine and it cured me." Listen to him! Look at him! When he says, "This poor man cried and the Lord heard him and delivered him out of all his troubles," don't accuse him of being a fool; and don't accuse him right away of being a liar. Give him the benefit at least of a good luck. Who is this man? Consider the character of these people and ask yourself this question: might they be telling the truth? That would fit better than any other suggestions you can have. This is building up the background for a person to have enough confidence in the medicine to take it.

There is another aspect. If you are seriously trying to decide whether or not the Bible is the Word of God, I would remind you that the God who is claimed to be the God of the Bible is a living Being. If the Bible is true, then God is alive. If God is alive, He knows you. He knows your heart. If God is alive and you are wondering about the Bible and He wants you to have confidence in it, don't you expect that He would move your heart toward it?

I am going to ask you to do this: recognize in yourself your own inner leading. When you honestly look at the Bible and add up the testimony about the Bible, do you have any hunches about it? Do you have any inner leading to suggest to you that all these various evidences could be easily understood if you would just accept the idea that the

Bible is what it claims to be—the revelation of the will of
God? If the Bible is at all true, remember, there is a living
God; and if there is a living God, you can be sure that in
kindness, mercy, and grace He will actually be working in
you. You may feel that that is intuition. Many things come
to you that way. In your ordinary, everyday business (especially if you happen to be in school and you have been
working mathematical problems in algebra, geometry, or
some such difficult area) would you mean to tell me you
don't go by hunches? Don't businessmen make use of ideas
that come to them?

If God is a living God, wouldn't it be proper to think
that He is an infinite person and that He is interested in
even me? If He is at all kind and merciful, would He not
give me some sort of guidance? How do you feel inwardly
led when you consider all these things? Consider the testimony of the Bible in the world at large, the effect that it
has had upon society as a whole and the actual witness of
believers themselves. If you feel in your heart that it could
very well be true, why not follow through on that?

Now take a look at the Bible yourself. I think you have
had enough of a look at it through what I have said to war-
rant opening it up and reading it. Try to read it intelligently. Don't read it just blindly. Try to find out what it
is supposed to be saying and look into it. Taste it for yourself. You can start in different places; it won't make too
much difference where you look. You will find some of the
stories that have to do with historical events of long ago,
and you will find them strange. You will read of worship
procedure, and you will find that strange. You will also
find human interest situations and descriptions of things
as they actually are happening. Read along in it and see
how it will affect your mind.

When you are looking at the Bible and "tasting" it, call
to mind the people whom you know. Do you know anybody who believes the Bible? Consider him. Do you know

anybody who doesn't believe it? Take a look at that person. Compare these two people. Consider which one you would want to line up with.

Do you know of anybody who criticizes the Bible? Do you know anybody who honors and respects it? Take a look at those two people. What kind of persons are they? Evaluate the testimony of such people; and when you are taking this look at it, decide for yourself if this is the kind of medicine you want to take. After you have looked at it I could ask you: do you have any reasonable objection now to at least looking into the Bible? Do you have confidence enough to take a dose of this medicine for yourself?

How sick are you? How distressed and burdened are you? I could ask you as the Lord Jesus asked the man who was lying paralyzed on a bed, "Wilt thou be made whole" (John 5:6)? Do you really want to be healed? If you do, I would suggest to you a very simple thing: do what the Bible says. Just obey it.

Perhaps you may wonder why we have sought confidence *about the Bible* rather than confidence *in the Bible*. We have gone round-about-it in trying to show you that the Bible in the world, in the testimony of other people, in its relation to its effectiveness and to its works would commend itself to you, but we haven't opened it yet. Why have we sought confidence *about the Bible* rather than seeking confidence *in the Bible?*

I have been largely guided in my thinking by what happened when the Lord Jesus was here upon earth. He was the incarnate Word of God; yet confidence in Him that Jesus of Nazareth was the Christ, the Son of the living God, was never grounded in any evaluation of Jesus of Nazareth as a man. I feel personally that the problem of accepting the Bible as the Word of God is parallel to the problem that people had in accepting Jesus of Nazareth as the Son of God. When anybody accepted Jesus of Nazareth in the New Testament as the Son of God, he did not do it only by looking at Him. You do not come to have confidence in the Bible by opening it up and looking into it. You could look at a doctor as long as you wanted to, and I don't know that you would have good ground for having confidence in him, but you could ask his patients and get confidence.

Some persons in the time of our Lord Jesus Christ gained confidence in Him and believed in Him. However, there is no case on record of anyone accepting Him as the Messiah or as the Christ by examining Him critically. He never attempted to win confidence by comparing Himself to other people or comparing His teaching with the teaching of other people. This leads me to think that no one will ever arrive at confidence in the Bible as the Word of God by studying that text in a critical approach or as an intellectual discipline. Reading the Bible will help, but it is not enough to build acceptance, to enable the soul to trust it as the Word of God. Even John the Baptist did not know Jesus of Nazareth was the Christ until after His baptism, when he saw the Holy Spirit coming upon Him and heard the voice from Heaven saying, "This is my beloved Son, in whom I am well pleased" (Matthew 3:17). It is when we know how the Bible has been endorsed by God that we find we can receive it as the Word of God.

This insight was clearly set forth by our Lord when He outlined the procedure by which men can come to receive Him as the Son of God. In John 5:31–47 the Lord Jesus pointed out that His hearers could come to believe in Him not by listening to Him, but by remembering the witness of John the Baptist, the works that Christ Himself had performed, the voice from Heaven that had identified Him, and the Scriptures themselves, which testified that He was the Christ. At no point in this presentation does the Lord present Himself as a man to be esteemed above all other men by comparison with them.

This is why I feel that the Bible will never be received in the heart as the Word of God by being studied in comparison with other books. I think it will be with you and the Bible as it was with Christ Jesus and His followers. You will believe on Him for the very work's sake. *You will come to believe in the Bible because of its effectiveness wherever it is received.*

CHAPTER 11

Building Confidence

How can a man increase his confidence in the Bible? How can anybody develop his feeling of assurance that the Bible is the Word of God?

Confidence in the Bible can grow. When a person begins to think that the Bible is true to the point where he will commit himself to it, he may not have all the confidence that is possible or even desirable. Think of a person—myself—as a sick man. I may go to a doctor because I am sick. I may have misgivings and uncertainty. I may go with a good deal of pessimism. The Lord Jesus once said to a man whose son was sick, "If thou canst believe, all things are possible to him that believeth." The father cried out, "Lord, I believe; help thou mine unbelief" (Mark 9:23–24). It is possible for a person to believe in the Bible and believe in the Lord Jesus Christ while still having a good deal of unbelief and uncertainty in his heart. But even as my confidence in the doctor can grow, so my confidence in the Bible can grow.

There are things that I could do, steps which I could take, which would strengthen my confidence in the doctor. When I go to him at his clinic or office, I might notice his equipment. If it looks efficient I could be impressed by that. If his manner is sure and confident, it would give evidence that he knows what he is doing. I could listen to what men say about him. I am already going to him, and I am taking his medicine; but I could be listening to what other people say about him and gain more and more confidence in him. I could check up on the opinions of former patients who say they believe in him. I could go and look at them and see. I could observe closely how his treatment affects me. He begins to treat me by giving me some medication. After I have taken it for a week or two and certain results happen in me, that would increase my confidence in the doctor.

When a man accepts the Bible as true, what other problems might he have? I do not expect that it would be about the validity of the Ten Commandments. Anybody who has read the Ten Commandments and has tried to keep them would say that those Commandments are right and just. I don't think that the difficulty would concern the desirability of "The Golden Rule." We might not think of it as practical, but we wouldn't say it was wrong. It is the real crux of the Gospel that gives us our problem: will God, as a person, operate supernaturally to the saving of the sinner?

It breaks down into such specific questions as these: is God really a person? Is God omniscient; does He know everything? Is He omnipotent; can He do anything? Will God judge, and in judgment will He destroy? In other words, is hell real? Will God accept substitution and sacrifice? Is it true that a sinner can come before God and confess his sins and that a sacrifice will be accepted by God in place of himself?

It is this sort of thinking that could trouble me, and I might wonder if any of this is true. Will God transfer my guilt to an innocent person, the Lord Jesus Christ, and transfer His righteousness to me so that, although I did not earn it, I may have the righteousness of the Lord Jesus Christ covering me like a garment, as a free gift? That is a wonderful idea, but is it true?

Will God really raise the dead? That is what the Bible says. Will God raise up men and keep them forever in Heaven? Is the new birth really necessary? Is it true you must be born again? Wouldn't it be all right if you were just good? Is the Holy Spirit a person? Is there such a thing as being guided and directed by the Holy Spirit? Can you grieve the Holy Spirit? Does He come into the heart? Am I to make room for Him? Does God answer prayer? Does it make any difference when I pray? These are questions that could come up if I am going to believe the Bible.

These items can never be proven separately one by one. As you have followed my thought, you will recognize that we are at the place where we are considering accepting the Bible as a whole as the revelation of God. We can feel from all the evidence on the outside that it is an important book and that the truth of God may well be in this book. We pick it up as it is. However, we have misgivings about it: we are not sure, but we start to read it. This then is our problem: are these things really so? We cannot pick any one of the questions by itself, take it out into the world and prove it. If we wait until we have every one of these questions solved, we will never believe. But there is a way of arriving at greater confidence.

Let us take another look, a long look, a repeated look, at the impact of the Gospel upon men everywhere. The Bible which we have in our hands implies all the things I have questioned. This book contains the message that God is a living Being, a person in Heaven, dealing with us here on earth in a supernatural fashion. Is this really so?

Now let us take this long look at the impact of the Gospel in the world, upon men anywhere and everywhere. Consider missions. Are they worthwhile? Does anything really happen on the mission field? What do people say who have been over there and looked? This book is the book the missionaries have. Listen to the missionaries. Let them report to you what happens when they tell the Gospel of the living God, the Gospel of judgment unto death, the Gospel of Heaven and hell, the Gospel of being born again by the grace of God through Christ Jesus, the Gospel of being saved by the substitutionary sacrifice of the Lord Jesus Christ (God will receive you freely to Himself and adopt you as a member of His family because Christ Jesus died for you). Let them report to you how it works through them.

If you should ever hear a negative voice, take a good look at that person. Does he know? Has he ever seen the situation? You will invariably find that the people (even unbelieving people) who know the facts on the mission fields are astonished at the effect of the Gospel on pagan peoples anywhere in the world. The Gospel comes from the Bible.

If you do not have a chance to listen to missionaries, I would say to you, *read.* If you want to have confidence in the Bible, ask someone to recommend a book on missionary life to you. Get some of the biographies of great missionaries. Read them and see what the Bible meant to those persons. Your confidence in the Bible will grow when you see how the Bible has been employed. These missionaries have had people come to them in fear, in bondage, and in weakness. Such may have been people who never heard the Gospel before. The missionaries tell them the story. The people listen and believe, and then are affected in notable fashion.

While we are looking at the impact of the Gospel, consider Christianity and the reality of "hypocrites." After all, there may be much in Christianity that you won't like. There may be much in the local church that you won't like; but look a little more closely. Are there many people in the local church who aren't real Christians? What does the existence of the "hypocrite" prove? Does this prove that the Gospel is wrong or ineffectual; or does it actually indicate that the benefits of the Gospel are so desirable, so much so that some people will imitate, hoping that they will also get these things? Add up all the cultural benefits of the true Gospel to people who really believe. When you are considering Christianity as a whole, don't get blocked behind some hypocrite. Step out on the side and look over the world as a whole. Look at the orphanages that Christians have prepared. Look at the hospitals, the leprosariums, the homes for incurables. Consider the schools they have organized and the education that they promote. Take a look at these things when you are asking yourself whether or not the Bible is reliable.

Let us take one more look. Is the Bible effectual among men? Are you acquainted with any notable converts? Do you know anybody at all who has ever really had a profound conversion? Do you know anybody who at one time was addicted to some habit, perhaps an alcoholic whose life was being ruined, whose home was torn apart, whose business was gone? Do you know anybody who was in such circumstances and then was really converted? Do you know of people who lived in darkness and in sin and were brought into a new life of virtue? I hope you do. Listen to their testimony. When you hear those people talk, listen to what they have to say about the Bible. Is the Bible meaningful to them?

If you hear one such person talk, it will be helpful. If you hear *two* people talk, it will be better. If you hear *three* people express confidence, it will be better still.

If no such testimony meetings are ever held in your own church, find a place where these meetings are held. If there are any places in your community where Christians get together and talk about what the Lord has done for them, go and listen. It is your soul that is at stake. When you listen to these people, ask yourself these questions: are they sincere? are they telling the truth? is the Bible really that helpful?

If you are not sure that you can ever become personally

acquainted with a real Christian with an imposing or a vivid testimony, go to the biographies of Christians. Ask someone to tell you what they consider to be the best story of a man who has experienced conversion and become a Christian. Get that book and read it. Read other testimonies of men who lived by faith. Every now and again someone will write a book telling what it has meant to him to believe in the Lord Jesus Christ.

What you are interested in in any reading or listening you may do is this: what do these people say about the Bible? How do they handle the Bible?

Consider Christianity as a whole: abroad on the foreign field, in all history, among Christians, and among people whom you know. Ask yourself about the impact of the Christian message, and then bring up the Bible and ask how the Bible relates to these things and how it is effective.

Another general line that you can follow is this: attend the preaching and teaching of the Bible by men who believe. Whether they are in your denomination or not, go and hear them. Your life and your soul are at stake. You do not have to join their denomination, but they are all servants of the Lord, and they are in the world for a purpose. They are lights shining to guide you on your pathway. Listen to them. Visit the services of such persons. No matter what town you live in, there is surely some preacher there who honors the Scriptures. Go listen to him. When it comes to Bible study, surely there is a Bible teacher somewhere in your community who teaches the Bible as if it is the Word of God. Stay around people who believe the Bible. You may not agree with every interpretation they offer, but what I am talking about is more elemental than interpretation. I am referring to an attitude.

When a revival service comes to your community, and if it is a service with any power at all, the man who is leading it believes the Bible. Certainly the great evangelists have all been men of the Book. They have held up the Bible saying, "Thus saith the Lord." "The Bible says" is their common phrase. Listen to them preach. Listen to them as they apply this truth to life round about them, and as you listen your faith will grow. Stop at the street corner and listen to street preachers. Go over to some denomination where you ordinarily do not attend. Do they have anyone preaching there that believes the Bible?

If you are truly interested in having a greater faith in the Bible, go listen to somebody who believes it, because God has a way of blessing preaching. You will find some in your denomination. Somewhere in your church there are men and women who really do believe the Bible. Associate with them, and listen to them.

I want to put in a negative word here. Avoid those preachers who are notorious for their uncertainty and unbelief. You might be caught once or twice listening to a man who doesn't believe, but there is no reason for you to invite yourself into it more and more.

If that preacher should happen to be your pastor in your own church, you are going to need help from God. While you are in the church services, turn your heart to the Lord and don't let the word of man get in there if you can possibly help it. But that is a problem all of its own and one which I would commend you to take to the Lord. When you have a choice in the matter, choose to go and listen to people who believe. If you want your faith to grow, mingle with people who believe.

In the same way, you can go to prayer meeting. Christian people pray. Especially people who really believe the Bible. They pray because the Bible promises them that if they ask they shall receive, if they seek they shall find, if they knock it shall be opened (Luke 11:9). The Bible tells them, ". . . ye have not, because ye ask not" (James 4:2). Such people actually want to have the help of God. They want the help of God upon their families, their homes, their children, their country, their church, their pastor, and themselves. They want the blessing of God upon missionaries, and upon the Gospel as it is preached over the whole wide world; and they pray, and pray, and pray. If you will go and share with these people and join with them in prayer, your own faith will grow.

What can you do to have your faith grow? Join with people at prayer meetings and in neighborhood Bible classes. If you will listen and if you will respond to the invitation from your friends there will be neighborhood Bible classes to attend. If it should be that there are no Bible classes in your community, why don't you start one? Why don't you invite your own friends with whom you are very close and with whom you feel comfortable to come to your home? You are going to open the Bible, read it, and see what it has to say to you. I'll promise you that your confidence in the Bible will grow.

In addition to all these things, keep reading the Bible. Read in the New Testament; read in the Gospels to see Jesus of Nazareth. The more you see Him, the more confidence you will have in Him; and the more confidence you have in Him, the more confidence you will have in the Bible. It is as simple as that.

I recently had a letter in the mail from a person who reminded me that I had told him to read in the New Testament and to read the Gospels. This man said, "I have been reading the Gospels, and it is better than it has ever been in my life as I read the Gospels and see Jesus of Nazareth."

Reading the New Testament in that way, with your eyes open, is as if you are mingling with people. It is like associating with the doctor. If he is a competent, capable, honest man, your confidence in him will grow.

Pray for more faith. The apostles said, "Lord, increase our faith" (Luke 17:5). In everything give thanks. Give thanks for all that God has shown you and ask Him to show you more. Let your requests be made known to God. Bring things to God in prayer. Ask and you shall receive,

seek and you shall find, knock and it shall be opened to
you. When you get answers to prayer, your confidence in
the Bible will grow more, and more, and more. Keep yourself in the presence of God. When you pick up His Book
in your hands, look up into His face and say, "Father, I
don't know any better. Show me Thy will." Open the Bible,
read it, and I will promise you that the living God will confirm it in your spirit, for His Spirit will bear witness with
your spirit that you are a child of God. Also, He will confirm in your heart the confidence that the Bible indeed is
the Word of God.

CHAPTER 12

How to Read the Bible

Generally speaking, getting to know the Bible is somewhat the same as getting to know a language. There is no better way to learn a language than to live in a home where the language is spoken. When missionaries want to acquire a dialect, they live in the community—in the very tents and homes—of people who speak the dialect. If you want to learn what is in the Bible, you need to read it and let the Bible speak to you, because in that way you will learn the language of the Bible.

Bible reading does not have to be haphazard and aimless. When a person has confidence in the Bible as being the authentic revelation from God, he should have a plan for reading. I think that one can intelligently plan Bible reading. I don't think any single plan by itself is the only way of going about it. But to help you get started, I am going to give you a plan which you can vary in any way you might want.

If I were starting out to get to know what is in the Bible, I would first read a Gospel. There is no reason why you shouldn't read the Gospel of Matthew. In reading the Gospel of Matthew, watch the Lord Jesus and mark the incidents in His life as they occur. I would suggest getting a Bible with paper that will stand marking and one that is not too expensive, so you won't mind marking it up. Then mark the paragraphs of each incident from where it starts to where it stops. Mark it in the margin so that you get the section. Don't go verse by verse entirely and certainly don't go by chapters, but put together all the different incidents as they are found. Don't take time to study all the possible ideas and every detail at first. Just read it through and especially watch the Lord Jesus. Get the broad outline of the story of each incident. Just watch the Lord Jesus. Listen to Him. When He says something, put yourself in the place of the people there and hear the words that He says. Notice the response to the Lord in each instance. What did the people do when He spoke? Notice also what happened when He dealt with the situation in that incident. What happened afterwards?

Thus, I would go through the Gospel of Matthew. I would not try to read it too quickly, but neither would I take long to read it. Get the overall picture. Stick with it from day to day until the Gospel of Matthew has been read through.

The second step would be to read the Acts of the Apostles. I would read it in the same manner as I did the Gospel of Matthew. Mark the incidents in the margin, noting where the incident starts and where it stops. Take note of what happened. Don't get bogged down in the long speeches that are recorded in the Book of Acts. You are going to come back to the speeches. You might read it through, but don't get weighted down in its possible meanings and don't try to understand it fully at this time. You just want to get acquainted with the facts of what actually happened.

As you are reading in the Acts of the Apostles, watch the work of the Holy Spirit. Here again, it would be profitable to mark every time the Holy Spirit is mentioned. Keep that before you. Don't take too long with those aspects of the stories that you can't see or understand. There will be things you don't know. Just as when you are learning to speak a language, there will be words you don't know, but you can't stop every conversation and make people explain each word. Listen to them. You will catch on to some of these things as you go along. This will take you a little while, too, because the Acts of the Apostles has twenty-eight chapters. You will have to listen to the words, but again read steadily so that you can get through with this book of the Acts of the Apostles.

The third step would be to read another Gospel. From the Book of Acts I would go back to the Gospel of Mark. I would treat it in the same way I treated the Gospel of Matthew. Watch the Lord Jesus. Mark the paragraphs of the incidents as they took place. Listen to what the Lord Jesus has to say, and note what the Lord Jesus does and the response of the people who saw Him and heard Him.

The fourth step would be to read the Acts of the Apostles. You say you have read them? You will never read them too often. Do you notice what I have done? I have suggested that you go back and take another look at the Lord Jesus Christ. Now, come and take another look at the Acts of the Apostles; and here I'll make this just a little different. In addition to what you have done before, mark the important names that you come across. There are names that you may remember. Again mark in the Bible any references to the Holy Spirit. You have already done something about that, but complete it. In addition, mark the instances of prayer. Make note of prayer in a special way wherever it happened. Draw your own mind and attention to it as you go along through the book of the Acts of the Apostles.

The fifth step would be to read another Gospel. Someone will point out that there is so much else in the Bible. I know, and we will come to that. You have read the Gospel of Matthew and then you have read the Book of Acts. You have read the Gospel of Mark and again you have read the Book of Acts. Now you are going to read the Gospel of

Luke. When you are reading the Gospel of Luke, mark everything that is a miracle. As you read, watch for the miraculous, everything that is superhuman. Mark every parable. Mark every opposition. Some people opposed the Lord Jesus. Notice who they were and what they said, and mark this in some way. If you want to use three different colored pencils or pens, you may mark everything that is a miracle with one color, every parable with another color, and every opposition with yet another color.

The sixth step I would suggest is to read the Book of the Acts. Must you read the Acts again? Yes, by all means. That is where the Church started. When you now read the Book of Acts, I want you to notice every case of opposition. You will be reading through the book for the third time, and by now you will be fairly familiar with its content. Now mark every case of opposition. In the first twelve chapters, notice what Peter does. From chapter thirteen on, notice what Paul does. Notice the opposition all the way through. By now you will be getting more familiar with it, and you will be learning something all the time.

The seventh step would be to read the Gospel of John. You have read Matthew, Mark and Luke. In reading the Gospel of John, I would suggest that you note each figure of speech used to refer to the Lord Jesus Christ. Note (underscore or circle with special color) every name given to the Lord Jesus Christ. "In the beginning was the Word" (John 1:1). "And the Word was made flesh" (John 1:14). Circle "the Word." "Behold the Lamb of God" (John 1:29). Circle "the Lamb of God." "I am the light of the world" (John 9:5). Circle "the light of the world." "I am the bread of life" (John 6:48). Circle "the bread of life." Go through this book chapter by chapter, and as you read note each figure of speech, every reference to the Lord Jesus Christ.

In addition, as you read the Gospel of John, note each incident which tells of men coming to faith. As a matter of fact, John will tell you, "And many other signs truly did Jesus in the presence of his disciples, which are not written in this book: but these are written, that ye might believe that Jesus is the Christ, the Son of God; and that believing ye might have life through his name" (John 20:30–31). Make a note in the margin whenever you see where a person came to faith.

There are also incidents where people turned away. I want you also to notice these. This is the advantage of using colored pencil or pen: because with different colors you can draw a contrast one from the other.

Now the eighth step, and again you are almost ready for what I am going to say, read the Book of the Acts. Now you will have read the four Gospels and you will have read the Acts four times. This is a good way to get oriented to the basic ideas of what the Christian Church is really all about. When you read the Book of the Acts this time, read the sermons carefully; take time to give a topic to each one. What is Peter saying on Pentecost? What is Peter saying when he stands before the council? I also want you to notice each conversation, each incident of a person coming to faith in Christ. Sometimes a number of people came and at other times individuals. Make it a point to be very sure to get those individual persons who began to believe. In the same way notice each case of persons turning away from the Gospel, because there were people who turned away from the Gospel even in the Book of the Acts.

You will now have read the four Gospels rather carefully, doing something with them as you are reading; and you will have read the Book of the Acts four times. This will give you a fairly thorough grasp of these five books.

I think you could profit now if you would use some organized aids to Bible study. Here are some books you may want to secure: (1) a handbook. Ask someone to recommend the name of a good handbook to the Bible. (2) Acquire a Bible atlas. An atlas will give you the geography of the countries and location of the cities. (3) Get a Bible dictionary. A one-volume Bible dictionary is not expensive and contains a tremendous amount of information. If you happen to notice a certain name or idea and wonder what it means, you can consult the Bible dictionary and get a clearer idea. (4) If you are able to afford it, get an encyclopedia in addition to the dictionary.

In selecting these reference books, take a look at them before you buy them. It may be that the print doesn't suit your eyes. If the print is too small and your eyesight is such that small print bothers you, it would be very foolish for you to get these books and never use them. It would be better for you to get a commentary in four volumes with large print than in two volumes with small print. These tools will be useful to you as you enter into your Bible reading.

In everything I have had to say about this guide to Bible reading, I have in mind that you will want to be reading in the Bible regularly for devotional purposes. You may read the portion you like or the portion you are interested in. But I am more concerned with seeking to share with you suggestions that will lead you to a study course of the Bible.

After you have read the four Gospels and the Book of the Acts four times, you still have much reading to do. You will profit by reading the introduction to each book in the handbook before reading the book itself. I would suggest that you now start reading in the Old Testament. If you are going to read the Book of Genesis, take the handbook and read what the author has to say about the Book of Genesis and then read the book itself.

I would not suggest a commentary on Genesis. A commentary is a book that contains explanations of the book; a handbook will just simply gather together the ideas that are in the book; a good handbook is not a commentary. The reason I do think you should not use a commentary at this point is that I want you to read the Bible. I want it to get to you. If you are going to have to teach Sunday School, you may want to use a commentary; but if you don't have to teach Sunday School and you are just reading for your own soul's sake, read the best—read the Scriptures. Never read the commentary first; read the Bible first.

I would say read an Old Testament book, and when you have finished reading it, after you have read the handbook introduction, then reread it just to get the story, just to find out what is in there. When you have finished the Old Testament book of Genesis, read a New Testament book. I would read the Gospel of Matthew. Read it without too much pressure on any particular study point. You can study that point later and separately. Get the idea again in view of what you read in Genesis. Having finished reading Matthew, I would suggest you go back and read another Old Testament book—the Book of Exodus. I would read the Book of Exodus through and follow it with a New Testament book—the book of the Acts of the Apostles. When you have finished reading the Book of the Acts go back to the Old Testament and read the Book of Leviticus. (As I have suggested, each time take the handbook and read the introduction to the book to find out in general what people say is in the book and then read the book itself.) When you have finished reading the Book of Leviticus, read another New Testament book—I Corinthians. Of course, you could read Romans, but I would suggest I Corinthians after reading the Book of Leviticus. After you have read I Corinthians, go back and read another Old Testament book— the Book of Numbers. Then come over into the New Testament and read a Gospel—the Gospel of Mark. If you look over this list, you will see a fairly consistent pattern alternating between the Old Testament and the New Testament.

In addition to the handbook, I would also use the atlas. Look up the names of the places that are mentioned and become familiar with them. The Bible dictionary will tell you about some of the characters and some of the things that were done. As you read about the temple, look up in the dictionary and see what it has to say about the temple. In that way you will gradually get to know what the Bible actually tells about.

When your study becomes regular, and you are going rather slowly because you are using your tools—handbook, atlas, and dictionary—in conjunction with your reading, you may want to do some broad, rapid reading for devotional use. In that connection, the handbook will help you to know what to expect. You can get acquainted with the various books of the Bible by reading what is given in the handbook. You should get to know what you could expect in Colossians, Ephesians, Philippians, II Peter, or II John.

By the end of the first year, you should get to know something of the landscape of the Bible. You should know that the first five books are called the Pentateuch. The books called history follow—Joshua, Judges, Ruth, I and II Samuel, I and II Kings, I and II Chronicles, Ezra, Nehemiah, and Esther. The next group of books is commonly called the poetical books of the Bible—Job, Psalms, Proverbs, Ecclesiastes, and Song of Solomon. The books of prophecy— the Major Prophets and the Minor Prophets—conclude the Old Testament. The New Testament begins with the four Gospels—Matthew, Mark, Luke, and John—followed by the Book of the Acts. Then you have the Epistles.

Let me point out to you that for your own devotional ideas, you may want to find language for prayer. Perhaps you feel in your heart you would like to pray more, but you don't really know what to say. Read the Psalms. Assign yourself a portion of the Psalms to read each day for devotion. They make good praying language.

If you want to understand more about men and human conduct, read Proverbs, Ecclesiastes, and Song of Solomon.

If you want to follow through to get a clear walk with the Lord so that you are conscious of His presence, get close to the Gospels. They will show you the Lord Jesus Christ; and as you are following along with Him, you will be blessed in Him.

If you would like to cultivate your confidence in prayer and become more and more of a praying person, keep reading in the Book of the Acts, because those people actually had God dealing with them, and this book will give you many instances of prayer that will stir your heart.

Perhaps you would like to understand more of your life in the Spirit. What does it mean to live as a believer? Read the Epistles. They were written to believers to help them understand the life in Christ.

If you would like to know more about Jesus Christ as He is now, read the Book of Revelation.

As you read this way in Scripture, mark the helpful passages. Here again, if you have a Bible that you can mark, use your own system; but you should have some passages that are really helpful to you, to which you will want to come back and feast on. As you find passages to help you and guide you in your praying, mark these inspiring promises. When reading, you will notice various passages which are "promises." Mark them so that you can come back to them in prayer and you will get better acquainted with them in that way. For instance, if you feel discouraged and in your Bible reading you come across some passage that seems to strengthen you, mark that passage.

In general while you are reading in the Old Testament, remember that history and prophecy deal with the nation of Israel. Watch for Israel. You will read of kings, and priests, and prophets, but you watch for Israel and keep track of its fortunes because it is a very important thing. What God did to Israel is a picture of what He will do with His Church.

In the Old Testament poetical books—Job, Psalms, Proverbs, Ecclesiastes, and Song of Solomon—watch for the heart and the mind of the writer and see how you are affected. When you get to the Gospels, watch for the Lord Jesus Christ in person, walking as a human being on earth. In the Book of the Acts, watch for the Holy Spirit and the Church. You will see Peter in the first twelve chapters and you will meet Paul in the last sixteen chapters, but watch for the work of the Holy Spirit and for the significance of the Church. In the Epistles watch for the believer living the life of God in Christ Jesus.

When you open the Bible, remember that it is God who inspired it, and you want to know about God. Acknowledge that you have not been what you ought to be; leave your heart and mind open for the grace of God. If you have not previously accepted Christ as Saviour, do so now. You may already have accepted Him as your Saviour; accept Him now as your Lord. Put your hand in His as you read the Bible and let Him lead you in the interpretation of it that you may receive the Holy Spirit and yield yourself to the indwelling Holy Spirit of God and obey the Lord. About anything that you have in mind to do, obey Him, so that in your heart and mind the disposition will be to do His will. He will show you more if you will do it that way. Hope in His mercy.

Over all, in all, and through all, love God and love man. You may say that you thought I was talking about Bible reading. I am. That is the frame of mind and heart in which the Bible can become more meaningful to you. It was given to be a lamp to your feet and a light on your pathway (Psalm 119:105), and *it will be* as *you enter into it* and *let it enter into you* and guide you along the way.